INSIDE THE MINDS SERIES

Inside the Minds:
Venture Capitalists
Inside the High Stakes and Fast Moving World of Venture Capital

eBrandedBooks.com
Get Published!

Published by eBrandedBooks.com, Inc.
For information on bulk orders or any other questions please email info@ebrandedbooks.com.

First Printing, May 2000
10 9 8 7 6 5 4 3 2 1

ISBN 1-58762-001-4

Library of Congress Card Number: 00-102627

Material in this book is for educational purposes only. This book is sold with the understanding that neither any of the interviewees or the publisher is engaged in rendering legal, accounting, investment, or any other professional service. The information in this book does not provide any guarantees in any way, shape, or form of securing a venture capital investment from any of the interviewees or any other sources.

This book is printed on acid free paper.

eBrandedBooks.com

Presents the

INSIDE THE MINDS SERIES

Inside the Minds: Venture Capitalists is the first book in the Inside the Minds Series. Other books currently include *Internet CFOs, Internet Marketing, Internet BizDev, Internet Bigwigs, Chief Technology Officers,* and *Internet Lawyers.* The series was conceived in order to give individuals worldwide actual insights into the leading minds of the Internet and technology revolution. Because individuals in this industry especially are so busy and the nature of their business is changing so quickly, there exist very few books that are published in a timely enough manner and written by individuals actually in industry. eBrandedBooks.com is now expanding the series to share the wealth of knowledge locked inside the minds of leading executives in every industry worldwide.

To nominate yourself or an executive level individual for an upcoming book in the Inside the Minds Series please email jennifer@ebrandedbooks.com. We are currently accepting nominations for executives worldwide in every major industry.

About eBrandedBooks.com

eBrandedBooks.com is the first ever print and electronic publisher to offer a free publishing solution for individuals and businesses worldwide. Individuals can publish a book, newsletter, article, group story, diary, research report, short story, play, and notes on any topic via the eBrandedBooks.com web site. eBrandedBooks.com acts as their personal agent and publisher: publishing their work electronically on eBrandedBooks.com, getting their work listed in other electronic marketplaces, promoting it with extensive advertising and affiliate programs, and simplifying the entire process for them. And if their work is purchased on eBrandedBooks.com 100 times, eBrandedBooks.com will edit, print publish, and help get it into bookstores and other retail outlets nationwide either as its own book or combined with other shorter works. eBrandedBooks.com also works with companies to help them write books, establish their own private label book publishing arms, and harness the written works of their community members. eBrandedBooks.com also publishes the highly acclaimed Inside the Minds series, Gold Digger series, and CEO series. For more information on becoming an eBrandedBooks.com business partner please email jonp@ebrandedbooks.com. For more information on becoming a published author please register at www.ebrandedbooks.com.

strategies, joint ventures, and where the future of Internet business development is heading among numerous other issues. *Inside the Minds: Internet BizDev* contains the most up to date information available regarding business development and is a must have for every executive, entrepreneur, and anyone in the business development or marketing world. (May 2000) $27.95

Inside the Minds: Internet Lawyers

The Most Up to Date Handbook of Important Answers to Issues Facing Every Entrepreneur, Lawyer, and Anyone with a Web Site — *Inside the Minds: Internet Lawyers* includes interviews with leading lawyers from some of the top Internet and technology focused law firms in the world. Their research and advice provide the most up to date information available on legal issues reshaping the laws that govern the Internet and anyone who uses it. Also examined are topics such as structuring ownership, raising money, venture capital, patents, intellectual property, forming the board, product liability, human resources, going public, stock options, partnership contracts, privacy, and other issues that every business (and their lawyers) should be aware of. *Inside the Minds: Internet Lawyers* contains the most up to date legal information available anywhere and is a must have for every entrepreneur, lawyer, and anyone with a web site. (June 2000) $27.95

Inside the Minds: Chief Technology Officers

Industry Experts Reveal the Secrets to Developing, Implementing, and Capitalizing on the Best Technologies in the World - *Inside the Minds: Chief Technology Officers* includes interviews with leading technology executives from some of the top Internet and technology companies in the world. Their experiences, advice, and research provide an unprecedented look at the various strategies involved with developing, implementing, and capitalizing on the best technologies in the world for companies of every size and in every industry. These experts also provide insider knowledge on the future technologies that will once again reshape the "wired world." *Inside the Minds: Chief Technology Officers* contains the most up to date information available and is a must have for every techie, entrepreneur, executive, and any one with an interest in the technology fueling the Internet and technology revolution. (June 2000) $27.95

The Entire Inside the Minds Series

The Most Comprehensive Set of Industry Experts Ever Reveal the Secrets
Inside the Minds: Venture Capitalists
Inside the Minds: Internet CFOs
Inside the Minds: Internet Bigwigs
Inside the Minds: Internet Marketing
Inside the Minds: Internet Bizdev
Inside the Minds: Internet Lawyers
Inside the Minds: Chief Technology Officers
(May, June 2000) $195.65

ORDER THESE OTHER GREAT BOOKS TODAY!

Great for Yourself or Send as a Gift to Someone Else!

Tear Out This Page and Mail or Fax To:

eBrandedBooks.com, PO Box 883, Bedford, MA 01730
or
Fax to (617) 249-1970

Name:

Email:

Shipping Address:

City: State: Zip:

Billing Address:

City: State: Zip:

Phone:

Internet Marketing: Venture Capitalists: Internet Bigwigs:

Internet CFOs: Internet :Lawyers: Internet BizDev:

Chief Technology Officers: Entire Series:

Total Number of Books (an entire series is counted as one):

Credit Card Type (Visa & Mastercard ONLY):

Credit Card Number:

Expiration Date:

Signature:

*(Please note the billing address much match the address on file with your credit card company exactly)

Please make sure to provide your email address!

We shall send a confirmation receipt to your email address. Shipping and handling charges of $3.95 per book and appropriate state tax charges will be applied. All books are paperback and will be shipped as soon as they become available. Sorry, no returns or refunds. Books that are not already published will be shipped upon publication date. Publication dates are subject to delay.

CONTENTS

MICHAEL MORITZ
Sequoia Capital

Before joining Sequoia in 1986, Michael Moritz worked in a variety of positions at Time Warner and was a founder of Technologic Partners. Michael focuses on information technology investments and currently sits on the boards of some of the most prestigious Internet and technology companies in the world.

Sequoia Capital has invested in companies such as Cisco Systems, 3COM, Oracle Systems, Plumtree Software, Precept Software, Progress Software, Quarterdeck, Quickturn, Quote.com, RightPoint Software, RightWorks, Saba Software, Silicon Compilers, Stanford Technology, Summit Design, Symantec, Syndesis, Wayfarer, Valid Logic, Visigenic, VitalSigns, Access Magazine, Affinia, Ashford.com, AtWeb, AuctionWatch.com, BenefitPoint, BuyProduce.com, Chipshot.com, Desktop.com, diCarta, eALITY, eGroups, E-Loan, eToys, EventSource.com, Freei.net, Global Center, Google, HomeWarehouse.com, InPurchase, International Network Services, Internet Wire, LinkExchange, Lipstream Networks, Medibuy, Miadora, Mini-Me Project, MP3.com, NextCard, Obongo, PartsAmerica.com, Perfecto Technologies, PlanetRX, Precept Software, RedEnvelope, Scient, SupplierMarket.com, Vividence, Wayfarer, WebSwap,

WebVan, X.com, Yahoo!, Yodlee.com, Altos, Apple Computer, Atari, Auspex Systems, Avid Technology, CADO, Cipher Data, Convex, Dysan, Network Appliance, Network Computing Devices, OneWorld Systems, Printronix, Pyramid, Radius, Starlight Networks, Storm Technology, Tandem, Tandon, VA Linux, Flextronics International, Global Center, and International Network Services.

Tell me a little bit why you think the venture capital world has received so much attention lately?

I think it's because the venture business is sitting in the center of the hurricane of change. Technology is intruding into more and more aspects of both the US and global economies. As new companies get formed to either go off in new directions or upset the equilibrium of existing businesses, the venture capital business becomes an integral part of all those changes. I think that to some degree it is a little surreal, especially because, in our businesses, we're not seeking publicity. People have this fascination with the markets, and although the venture businesses received attention in previous years, it is nothing compared to the extent it gets today. Every time there's tremendous buoyancy in a new company or the NASDAQ goes berserk over a venture-backed stock, the inevitable onslaught of media attention follows.

Tell me a little bit about how you got into venture capital.

My first job out of school was as a correspondent for *Time* magazine. I did that for about four years. I wrote a couple of books while I was at *Time*, one about the Chrysler company, and another about Apple computer. Eventually, I got bored. I knew when I went into journalism that I didn't want to do it for a long time, and felt that it was a fabulous way to have a very enjoyable period at the beginning of a career. I became tired with working at such a large company and saw how predictable the future was going to be if I stayed there. Then, together with a friend of mine who had been at the *Wall Street Journal*, we started a company called Technologic Partners. That was quite a long time ago now, maybe 16 years. We were partners in that for some time before I decided that it was too much like journalism, even though it was a small company. Through my work at *Time* and also at Technologic, I got to know a lot of people in the venture business and thought it looked like a fairly amusing diversion. I called a few people who I knew—or *had met* is probably a better description—in the venture business, including Don Valentine who is the founder of Sequoia Capital.

How has being a venture capitalist changed over the last number of years?

It relates to your first question: Nobody used to care about us. We occupied a very small space where our only visitors used to be people who worked between San Jose and San Francisco. On occasion, there were delegations of guys in blue suits from Japan who would leave us presents and disappear and nothing then would ever happen. Today for some reason, everybody wants to come and meet with us or do business with us in some fashion. The underlying pace of the business has sped up tremendously as a result of the Internet, and I think it's due to a couple of things. It's due to the increased platform of a number of investments that firms like Sequoia Capital and a short list of other firms have made. These investments have in turn spawned more investments, because each of these companies has frustrated entrepreneurs inside of them who want to do their own things. It becomes a self-fulfilling cycle of creation of new ventures. The second thing is that in the last few years the Internet has enabled huge investments in new media companies, financial service companies, and retailing companies—places where we never used to invest. Our bailiwick used to be very much the meat-and -potatoes technology, hard-core semi-conductors, subsystems, software equipment, and software companies. And that today is the platform upon which we build everything else. It's still the place that is the single most important area for us to continue investing, but it's also afforded us this incredible opportunity to go and compete with the likes of CBS, Time Warner, CitiBank, Toys R Us, and others.

Tell me a little bit about the investment philosophy of Sequoia Capital.

It's very simple and it has never changed. All we want to do is to find a new, fast growing market that offers the promise of being extremely large. We want a market where the impact or the effect of a change in technology will be profound, and we want to be the investor in the leading company in that new market.

What do you think are some of the best opportunities yet to be capitalized upon in the Internet?

I know this might sound a little funny, but I think the best opportunities are the ones that we really aren't thinking about. It's very easy in retrospect to say that we had a sense of the scope and size and magnitude of some of the really big winners—such as a Yahoo or a Cisco. But the fact of the matter is, I think, that we're always surprised by how large some of these new markets have become. When Cisco got started, nobody really understood how big that business was going to be—or at least very few people understood. I think the same is going to be true today for a bunch of people who wander off the Stanford or MIT campus or come out of a large company somewhere with an idea that will cause a profound shift in a marketplace.

When you're looking at potential ventures to back, what type of business models are you looking for? What are you specifically looking for in their business model?

We want to invest in a company where, once all the froth has disappeared from the surface, there is a wonderful business at the core. We'd always prefer to be an investor in a company that is a great business than in a company that is a great investment. Great businesses lead to great investments. Great investments don't necessarily spawn great companies.

How do you envision certain parts of the Internet—such as online advertising or e-commerce—changing over the next couple of years?

Several things will happen. Let's go with those two particular examples: advertising-based businesses and retailing businesses on the Internet. Both are going to be enormous businesses, even bigger than people imagine. But many of the companies that have already gotten started or will get started attacking both of those segments will fail, become insignificant footnotes, or emerge into other entities. Out of all this frenetic activity, there will definitely be a handful of extraordinary companies that become pillars of their respective industries for the next 20 years.

What do you think will surprise the general public the most about broadband access?

Well, I am just watching one small example of that right now: Yahoo! Finance Vision—streaming finance-focused video over the Internet—which was launched recently and is, in the grand scheme of things, a small example, but it gives you a taste of how our lives will be transformed. At home, people's habits are transformed as soon as they get DSL or a cable modem. They are then, at that point, connected to everything else in the world. Once you have DSL, it's extremely painful to have to connect to the Internet via a 56K modem or anything less. But more than that, it means that everyone and anything is immediately accessible, and that changes the way that individuals and businesses communicate. It changes the way they buy and sell things. I'm not for a moment saying that it's good, nor am I rendering any sort of judgment; it's just a fact about how it changes people's habits.

Do you think it's going to create a whole new wave of opportunities in terms of new ventures being started?

Yes, undoubtedly, because we're in a world where—in terms of technology—nothing is ever going to be fast enough.

For how long do you typically hold on to your investments?

We like to be investors in companies for a long time, so as individual general partners in Sequoia Capital, all of us own different stocks that we bought even as far back as 15 years ago—or longer. A couple of the guys here who were around in the late '70s or early '80s still own stock that was bought back then.

Tell me about some of your favorite investments.

Some of our favorite investments are ones that we've only made recently, but where we've been very intimately involved with a company since their formation—whether it was six weeks, five years, 10 years, or 15 years ago. WebVan is one that we've been very closely associated with since it got started. It's a company that is symbolic of the possibilities brought about by the Internet. There are not many companies in Silicon Valley or that have come out of

Silicon Valley that will have a big effect on young mothers as well as older people. WebVan has that opportunity.

There are a lot of semi-conductor and communication equipment companies that we have investments in as well. Avanex is a public company we invested in that makes optical networking equipment. For most people outside of the investment community, Avanex will be a mysterious sounding company whose products most people don't understand. However, without a company like Avanex, you and I don't get Yahoo! Finance Vision, and WebVan. So there are a lot of companies like that in which we have investments as sort of building-block companies, yet they won't have the kind of popular appeal of a WebVan or Shockwave.

How long do you think it will be before people get broadband access integrated into part of their everyday lives?

It's a very different story for individuals than it is for businesses. There will always be some segments of the population who won't use it nor have a need for it. There will be others who only use a particular aspect of it. Over time, however, it will be the sort of thing that is as taken for granted as electricity or the old dial-up telephones, and people won't think very much about it. They'll just take it for granted as the medium through which a service—that can be of great use to the public—is delivered.

Take me through some of the evaluation parameters or milestones that you look for when trying to value some of the companies you fund.

We don't use anything more complicated than the back of an envelope when we're doing an early-stage investment. It goes something like this: You have three constituencies— let's assume it's a startup company. You want to have a very interested, animated, enthusiastic set of shareholders. The shareholders are the founders, investors, and management team of the company. They all have to own enough of the company to care about the company. And getting the balance right is all there is to it. When we invest in a small enterprise—let's say it's just us and the founders to begin with—we always think about the way in which the pie needs to be cut. It needs to be divided three ways, and in a fashion that we all get roughly what we deserve and there are no ill feelings. When we talk to people about negotiating these sorts of things, we always say to the founders or to a prospective CEO that our goal should be to make sure that everybody is equally dissatisfied. We don't want to be in a situation where someone felt that he got a much better deal than he might have hoped for, and we don't want people, founders, management, or ourselves feeling that we got a raw deal. Life is too short. We really think of ourselves as partners in these enterprises for very long periods of time, and I think that is demonstrated by the length of time that we're very close to these companies. Now, our roles in the companies change over time, and we're not confused about the difference between being in the venture capital business and being an operating manager in a company. But if you talk to some of the companies that have had some of the better investors around Silicon Valley, they would say that the investors are part of their team.

When you're looking at making an investment in a company, are there specific things you're looking for, such as the quality of the management team or a proprietary technology?

Let's assume a little company has come in and convinced us that the market has the right characteristics. Then we're only looking for two things: We're looking for a product or service that makes a real difference to a customer, and we're looking for people with a passion.

There's so much talk about in the business-to-business marketplace right now. How hard it is for business-to-consumer companies to still get funded?

Let's define a business-to-consumer company. Business-to-consumer can be a lot of things. When people use the phrase business-to-consumer, what they're talking about are Internet-based retailers on the whole. Shockwave is a business-to-consumer company, in a way. It's an entertainment company providing a service to consumers. But I'm sure when you said business-to-consumer, you didn't think of companies like Shockwave; you were thinking more of companies like eToys or WebVan or some smaller retailers. Everybody is very busy throwing acronyms around these days. Are we going to stop financing companies that provide products and services? Absolutely not. Are we going to finance the fifteenth

Internet pet store? Absolutely not. Many people are off on a tangent about how business-to-consumer is such a dreadful business. If everybody had thought that in 1987, 11 years after the first personal computer company was formed, who would ever had thought it possible for a little personal computer company called Dell Computer to get started? It's never too late. When we financed Cisco, there were lots of other people and companies in the router business. A lot of our business is based on never saying never. Every time we make an investment in a company, it's always a journey against all odds, and it's always the founders against the world. Everybody is always betting against us and everybody is always saying it's impossible. So are we just being cautious about changing dynamics in particular markets? Yes. Are we totally and utterly intimidated by them? No.

Cisco and Dell are both interesting examples. When you are looking at a deal and there's already substantial competition in the marketplace for it, how are you looking for them to really differentiate themselves?

Well, they could have a different product. They could use different distribution channels. Part of the reason that Dell succeeded was that its original novel contribution was not the technology or the design of the computer, but there was an original insight about the way that it should be sold.

It's a tough thing to sell. It sounds like he was basically pitching his innovation and a different way to sell the product.

Well, nobody wanted to back them, and that's the reason Michael owned so much of his company. He had a brutal time. He had one of these barefoot journeys across the desert and his company nearly went out of business a couple of times. And everybody bet against him.

What creates value for startup Internet companies? Is it registered users, revenues, partnerships, or a combination thereof?

It depends a little bit on the business, but having a million users these days as an Internet company is a fairly meaningless statistic. A million isn't what it used to be, and, in fact, is a very small number. So if you're attacking Yahoo and you have a million users for example, is that meaningful? No. You don't have a prayer when you're going up against a company with 150 million users. So you have to put it in some sort of perspective. Usage numbers don't mean anything. To me, it's somewhat like a little company that's boasting about all the awards it got for its products, which may be wonderful, but we'd prefer to have a real viable business model and no awards.

You mentioned WebVan, which is an interesting example of an Internet company developing a significant off-line component to their business. Where do you see that trend going for other Internet based businesses?

There are not many purely digital businesses any more. But if you're in a business where a service or a product cannot be delivered via a telephone line, you need some sort of off-line component. You need to factor in a distribution center, call center, and other pieces of the puzzle.

Do you feel it's easier for a company that's essentially only been online to establish their off-line component, rather than vice versa?

If you force me into a yes or no answer, I'd say yes. Mostly because the online companies don't have as much baggage to contend with as some off-line companies, who probably have a history of 70 years in business and are suddenly faced with an abrupt change. For example, if you're the Proctor and Gamble Company and you're wondering about how to sell your goods online, how do you do that without irritating one of your existing retail customers?

How do you feel a market crash would affect the wave of new companies entering the marketplace?

It always takes time for a sudden down turn in the public markets to ripple back into the private markets. It can take as much as a year or two years, but eventually it will definitely have an effect. You can see that now among business-to-consumer retailers. Ever since Amazon.com caught a cold, it's much more difficult for entrepreneurs wishing to start an Internet-based retail company to get financed.

How much success do you think international dot coms will have in getting up and running quickly, and then expanding upon their presence?

It will vary. The big advantage an American dot com has is that it is getting started in the market that is the largest single market in the world. This is a significant advantage compared to getting started in Finland or Patagonia, and means that you have a lot of leverage in getting into additional markets. If you start in a small market and then try to get into much bigger markets, it's more challenging. So I have no problem understanding how a company gets started in Britain, France, Germany, or Italy and flourishes within its own market and adjacent geographies. However, I think it's tremendously challenging for a company born in Frankfurt or in London to become a global company—which isn't to say that it won't happen. But if you want to do a local version of Yahoo Germany or eBay Denmark, and then expand to compete worldwide, you're going to have problems. On the other hand, ICQ, the Instant Messaging software company that was born in Israel and sold to AOL, could absolutely have become a global company because it was ahead of all of its US competitors. If a small company starts outside of North America and really wants to flourish in a global fashion, it has to be in a market that is being ignored or missed by US companies, or else be dramatically ahead in their technology.

What about the hand-held and mobile devices in Europe, for example?

Well, you picked one example where Europe is clearly ahead of the US in terms of wireless services. It actually highlights a point I was making previously, because the benefit that the wireless companies have in Europe is that they have a homogenous platform on which to build their services, and it's a huge platform compared to North America. They have one large market platform and they are accruing those benefits. But then you say, okay, while this is a fabulous example of a fantastic market outside of North America, thinking of the next one or two is very difficult.

There's so much talk about so many other things than actual profits. But the Amazons and all the rest are eventually going to flip on their profit switches. Tell me about some of the Internet business models that you think will prove to be the most profitable in the long run.

Unless you have some sort of novelty brought about by the arrival of the Internet, there's no reason to believe that, in the long term, the dawn of the Internet means that a bad business off-line should suddenly be transformed into great business online. You will have margin structures of businesses on the Internet that are great and modest and poor, just as you do in the off-line world. Well-run media companies in the off-line world are fabulous profit generators. The same is true in the online world. Just take a look at Yahoo. There are some businesses where significant cost is taken out of the operating model by the online transformation, and those will inherently be more profitable than their off-line counterparts.

What industries in general do you think will be affected the most over the next couple of years?

It's across the board. If I were an investor or manager in any company where I had sets of intermediaries between the customer and me, my knees would be beginning to shake.

How do you personally keep on top of everything that's happening in the space?

I don't. I don't think one person can. I think you can as an organization, but so much is happening so quickly that it's asking a bit much for an individual to stay abreast of all the changes.

Tell me about some of the Internet companies that you admire the most for what they've done.

This will sound incredibly parochial, but I'll pick three in which we've invested: Cisco, Yahoo, and WebVan. Cisco because 13 years later, it is in the business that it began— the same one that its founders could describe to us 13 years ago. It's in the business of networking networks, and it's done so in a fashion that has surpassed everybody's expectations and provided real value to all of its customers—and, subsequently, their customers. They have done so in a fashion that has become a vehicle of admiration for everyone who is not part of that company. They have built one of the world's must stunning businesses.

If you'll excuse the insularity, in a different business at a different time, the same is true of Yahoo. Again, both those companies have been extraordinarily well managed. They've also had little turnover in the people. The people who run those companies have got an extraordinary passion for the businesses they're building. They haven't lost the need to serve their customers. The individuals have been able to keep their feet on the ground despite the sort of rush that surrounds them.

And WebVan, the youngest of that troika—well, the plan is so bold, the dream is so large, the challenge is so great, that if anyone three years ago had said that we'd be able to do what we've done, nobody would have believed us. The notion of being able to provide households and businesses with the products that they want when they want them sounds so simple, yet is so difficult to do.

Tell me a little bit of what you find the most exciting part of being a venture capitalist is.

Every day is composed of a hundred soap operas.

How has it changed in the last five years?

We see more soap opera episodes every day than we ever used to. It's like the difference between having network television and cable: You have a lot more channels. I can't imagine a more exhilarating place to live and to work.

HEIDI ROIZEN
SOFTBANK Venture Capital

Heidi Roizen joined SOFTBANK Venture Capital's technology fund in April 1999. Heidi is also an advisory board member of Time Domain Corporation, Garage.com, and is a member of the Stanford Board of Trustees Nominating Committee. Prior to joining SOFTBANK Venture Capital, Heidi was a consultant to numerous technology companies, indcluding Microsoft, Intel and Compaq. From 1996 to 1997, she was Vice President of Worldwide Developer Relations for Apple Computer. Heidi has been recognized as one of the 100 most influential people in the microcomputer industry by MicroTimes, Personal Computing Magazine and Upside Magazine.

Softbank Venture Capital has invested in companies such as Abuzz Technologies, Agentics, AnyDay.com, Art Technology Group, Art.com, Asia Online, Automated Trading Systems, beMANY!, BizBlast.com, Biztro, BlueLight.com, Broad Daylight, Buy.com, Career Central, ChannelWave Software, CharitableWay.com, Comergent Technologies, Communities.com, Connected, Critical Path, Decisive Technologies, Differential, Digimarc, DoDots, DrDrew.com, eCoverage, Electron Economy, E-LOAN, Email Publishing, eShare Technologies, Everest Broadband Networks, Exactis, FastParts, Finali,

Gamesville.com, GeoCities, HeyAnita.com, HotVoice, iChristian.com, Ignition, Impulse!Buy Network, Intend Change Group, Interliant, International ThinkLink, InterTrust Technologies, INVESTools, Invisible Worlds, iPrint.com, Legal Knowledge, Life Cycle Systems, MessageMedia, More.com, Net2Phone, NetMind Technologies, PayTrust.com, PENgroup.com, PeoplePC, PersonaLogic, PhotoPoint, planetU, Preview Systems, Prio, Proxinet, ReachCast, Reciprocal, Reelplay.com, Rentals.com, Service Metrics, ServiceMagic.com, ShareWave, Sonnet Financial, Spinway.com, StartSampling, Support.com, TelEvoke, TellSoft Technologies, Terabeam Networks, TheStreet.com, ThirdAge Media, Toysrus.com, Urban Media, USWeb/CKS, UTStarcom, VeriSign, Vstream, Yoyodyne Entertainment, and Zip2.

What do you like the best about being a venture capitalist?

As far as I'm concerned, I have the best job in the world. Here's how I explained it to my 80-year-old mother a few months ago: All day long, really smart people contact me and tell me about the dreams they have for building companies. If I like the people and their dreams, I get to buy part of the company and participate in its success—and I don't even have to spend my own money. Then, if the company is successful, I get to keep some of the returns. What could be better than this?

Okay—in truth, it isn't quite that simple. Of course, we at SOFTBANK have a huge commitment and fiduciary responsibility to the people whose money we invest—that is, the limited partners. We take great care when evaluating opportunities, and turn down 99 percent of the deals pitched to us. We do a tremendous amount of due diligence on the people, the market segment, the technology, and the competition before we invest. Once we do decide to invest, we work our butts off on the boards of these chosen companies, helping them plan, recruit, resolve conflicts, develop businesses, and conquer the myriad challenges that arise in an Internet company today. Our days are filled with meetings, briefings, dozens of phone calls, hundreds of emails—the inflow never seems to end. So, this is not a job for the 9-to-5er. I find the daily work exhilarating. Each day my mind is stretched by new markets or by new ways to look at traditional ones. The number of "ah-has" you can have—moments of insight and inspiration—are huge in this job. You really get an opportunity to pursue your interests in each of the companies you back.

Tell me about the team you work with at SOFTBANK.

Each of the managing directors of SOFTBANK was a "C"-level operating executive (CEO, CTO, CFO) prior to becoming a venture capitalist, so we've all been on the other side of the table. Furthermore, we all picked each other because of our common desires: to build great companies, to be entrepreneur-friendly, to execute ethical deals, and to have enough time left each day to spend a little time with our young children. Team dynamics are critical to a VC firm because each partner relies heavily on the work ethic, talents, and instincts of the others. We have assembled an awesome team.

What do you like the most about working with entrepreneurs?

Instead of being with one group of people, day in and day out, for years, I get to be involved with a dozen or so teams, playing the role of a virtual team member. Though the role is more coach than player, I still cherish the victories and seek further victory in the challenges. Because my number-one goal is to invest in CEOs more capable than I am, I get to learn from these tremendous business players as we tackle problems together.

This is not to say that every day is fun and easy. There are market downturns, competitors who come from nowhere with superior products, missed schedules, people who need to be fired, tragedies, unsolvable personality conflicts. People are not simple, and business can be very messy. You really have to be willing to walk in each day with your waders on, ready to get to the core of the problem and solve it—whatever it takes. Especially in the Internet economy is the maxim, "He who hesitates is creamed."

Is there anything you don't like about being a venture capitalist?

The only truly bad thing about this job is the pace. I got a business plan delivered to my home on Christmas Eve. I had people emailing me Christmas day, then angry that they didn't get an answer in 24 hours. Every entrepreneur is in a hurry, every fundraising is urgent, every person with a dream believes his dream is the best. I get about fifty incoming requests for funding a week, as do my partners, so that is about one thousand plans a month. Out of that, we'll fund maybe four, maybe six. So that leaves about 995 people who will walk away disappointed. That is hard for people to understand.

What are some of the basics entrepreneurs should understand about venture capitalists?

Perhaps that is the first and best lesson an entrepreneur can learn—VC firms are not government agencies compelled to respond in detail to every incoming request. Come to think of it, I don't know of any government agency that works that way either! VC firms are small collections of professionals: in our case, five investing partners, each with a "Netbatsu Development Officer" who works in concert with the partner to review incoming deals. This small team deals with an enormous influx of deals, a very small portion of which they can fund. They have to make quick decisions on whether to even read the business plan or not, decisions which may seem arbitrary to the entrepreneur. Venture capitalists are ultimately judged by one thing only: the financial return on the funds. They are not there to counsel the pitching entrepreneurs or help improve their plans, to give career advice or to make introductions into their portfolio—none of this, unless it helps one of their investments succeed. And they have to make these time-and-effort tradeoffs quickly, given the huge volume they receive of such requests.

So how do you make those tradeoffs and pick our investments?

Some of it is fund-specific. Our fund, for example, invests only in Internet companies. We chose this because of the growth we expect in the category and the expertise we've built internally. It is easier to help a company be successful when you have some deep domain knowledge in the market space or in the type of company being built. We also focus on areas where the individual partners have knowledge. For example, Brad Feld at SOFTBANK is probably one of the world's experts on messaging technologies, so he can easily evaluate messaging deals; with his expertise and portfolio, he can greatly help in ensuring their success.

Are there any specifics you look for in deals you invest in?

We have in place some filters that may seem arbitrary, like location, when in fact they are not arbitrary at all. We don't do deals outside the areas to which we're willing to travel regularly. Yes, we may miss out on some great deals in Boise, but that is a risk we've deemed necessary in order to do a truly great job as company builders. We need to have enough face-to-face opportunities to really help the team, and we can't do that given the realities of travel time. And, judging from results so far, there are more than enough deals in the areas we've chosen to focus on. As a result, many deals are rejected on the basis of geography alone. This does not mean they are not fundable, just not fundable by us.

Perhaps the most arbitrary filter of all—which I wish I had understood when I was first an entrepreneur raising money—is what I'll call "deal cadence." Just like how on the news, sometimes stories that wouldn't usually get covered end up on the air because it is a "slow news day." In the same vein, it's true that some deals get more attention because they were among a smaller incoming flow that week. This doesn't mean that a bad deal will get funded just because we're having a slower week. But all deals require quick responses, so the more deals you get in a week, the less time you have to devote to each one, and the more you'll have to reject out-of-hand. On the flip side, if one week produces a lot of good deals, we may be consumed for a few weeks after that taking those to their logical conclusions, so the new incoming deals get less attention. As a result, timing may be the most critical thing of all, and there is no way to predict what is good or bad timing. You can always be sure, however, that it's not a good idea to send deals in the week before Christmas!

Do you invest in all early stage companies or do you have a mix in your portfolio?

Most venture firms seek a certain portfolio balance—a certain percentage of early-stage deals, some later-stage, a few bets in each category, etc. We try not to make competitive investments so that our team is not torn between which deals to promote. A good deal could end up being turned down because we've already invested in someone with a similar plan, or because we've made a significant amount of later-stage bets and have deemed that, for portfolio balance, we need to now focus on early-stage deals exclusively.

If there is one lesson to take away from all the above, it is DON'T TAKE A REJECTION PERSONALLY. Frequently, when deals get turned down, it has nothing to do with the individual deal's merits. It's important not to lose hope: There are scads of venture capital firms, and being turned down by any one of them is not the end of the world!

How does your experience help you to invest in the right types of companies?

Truthfully, much of the skill in knowing what to look for is acquired from years of experience examining things, picking things, and observing how they ultimately do— both in your own investments and the ones you turn down that others take on. We can run lots of analyses against the business models presented to us, but that is only a small part of what we're looking for.

What types of information should entrepreneurs be submitting when looking for venture backing?

We've tried to be as entrepreneur-friendly as possible when it comes to navigating our process. We've enumerated and explained the steps on our website, www.sbvc.com. We ask that all submissions take place electronically via an executive summary, which is the first step. It should address the following, in about two pages:

1. What is your business?
2. What is your business model (primary source of revenue)?

3.What need are you fulfilling or what problem are you solving?

4.Who are your competitors?

5.Who are your customers?

6.What is the status of your development?

-Idea stage

-Development stage

-Product or service available to customers

-Have raised some revenue

-Have raised significant revenue and are looking to ramp up business

7.How much money are you looking to raise?

8.What is your target valuation?

9.Who are your current investors?

10.Where are you headquartered?

This information, coupled with information about you and your team, are what we use to determine whether we should take a meeting with you to hear your pitch. Remember, this summary shouldn't be competing in length with *War and Peace*—if it is, it won't get read. Just provide enough information to give us the gist of what you're trying to do and why you have a shot at being successful.

In reality, what are the chances of getting funded?

The reality is, 50 percent of the decision will be based on the person who's making the request: What is his or her background and experience? Is this a person who we know from prior work together? Does this person have a good reputation in the industry? It is painful to hear, but true: Most VCs back only people they know and respect, or people referred and endorsed by someone they know and respect. You can argue that this is unfair, but our job is not to be fair: Our job is to find and back great entrepreneurs who will bring great returns to the fund. There is a strong correlation between past and future successes, and much reduction of risk when we know personally or can check with high integrity the background of the person we're handing our money to.

If you are invited to make a presentation, how should you prepare?

If you are invited in to make a presentation, be prepared with a succinct and well-rehearsed pitch. It is rare that a person can come in and shoot from the hip without any materials and get funding. The lore is the deal done on one napkin, the reality is most of our investments come as the result of a compelling and well-organized presentation, taking all the points of the executive summary and expanding upon them.

Most VC firms will give you an hour-long meeting. I recommend that you hone the pitch down to half an hour so that there is plenty of time for conversation. Also, don't allow the VC to get you off course. I've seen meetings where one person in the room will get into a series of questions that are personally interesting to him but not germane to the investment. The entrepreneur, wishing to appear responsive, thoroughly answers each question, only to run out of time. If the VC you're pitching is like we are, meetings are tightly scheduled and we can't simply stay for another hour. A good entrepreneur controls the pitch meeting, including setting up the agenda and keeping to it.

Expect that you may have to give your presentation twice. Most VC firms operate on a certain level of consensus, and with each partner serving on eight to ten boards at any given time, not all of the partners can be at every meeting. So if you are asked back to repeat your performance, that is a good sign.

How do you approach the issue of valuation?

The question that usually comes up fairly quickly is "What valuation will I get?" Valuations are more an art than a science: We try to have all sorts of ways to value companies, but particularly with early-stage ones, it is a bit like pulling numbers out of a hat. Our advantage is that we price lots of deals every week, and we're in a competitive market where the market will ultimately decide, so even though this process is not very formulaic, I do believe that there are trends that put valuations of funded companies into recognizable bands.

More important than the valuation you get is how much of the company you give up before you get to a liquidity event, and what your stake looks like then. The highest valuation doesn't always mean the best deal. There are all sorts of terms and provisions that can make a $10 million pre-offer much worse than a $8 million pre-offer. It is critical that you engage an attorney on your side who understands venture law. Your attorney needs to be able to work with you to plot the terms of your deal into a meaningful spreadsheet that will help you evaluate the effect of the various terms in the potential outcomes you might achieve. It is also important to project the total funding necessary all the way through to an IPO, and understand how your stake will be diluted in each subsequent round. Be sure to allocate a sufficient percentage of the company (the rule of thumb today is 20 percent) for the employees you will be hiring. With all of these numbers plotted out, you can better understand what variables in the financing equation—valuation, liquidity preference, anti-dilution provisions, participation—are the most critical for you to focus on and negotiate.

How much do you normally invest in any given deal?

As for how much we invest, it really depends upon the company's needs and the opportunity at hand. We've invested as little as $250,000 or as much as $25 million in a first-round investment. Generally, a 'value-add' venture firm like SOFTBANK will not invest unless we can own a meaningful portion, something like 20 percent after financing. For us to apply our own time, brand, portfolio, and to generally commit to back you and not fund any competitor, we need to have enough of the company to justify the effort involved. We're happy to work with another venture firm if you'd like to have two investors, as long as you are comfortable with the dilution of having two investors. And we would expect to participate in further rounds of financing as you grow your company.

What about subsequent financing rounds?

When you go out for a subsequent round, you can choose to ask your VC to make a 'pre-emptive' offer, or you can 'price to market' with a new VC. A pre-emptive offer gives you the advantage of a quick turnaround with little management time and not a lot of dog-and-pony shows, and you don't have to introduce new investors to the scene. The downside, however, may be that you don't get the highest possible price, or that you don't bring on additional investors who can add other value beyond money, such as strategic alliances, domain knowledge, or simply the fact that if they invest in you, they won't back your competition. If you choose to 'price to market', it is best to first meet with your existing lead investor to ensure that they will take their share of the financing ("play pro-rata") when you do find a lead. Most companies like SOFTBANK will introduce you to the investors they feel will be the most attracted to what you are doing and the most able to help out.

What should you look for in your financing partner?

It has never felt truer than today that money is a commodity in Silicon Valley. There are literally billions of dollars chasing deals, everyone from professional VCs to angels to sports professionals and real estate developers. If you have a fundable business, someone will likely fund it. Unfortunately, some un-fundable businesses will get funding too, but that is a temporary phenomenon.

To me, the source of the money is far more important than the valuation, within reason. Think of your investor as someone you are hiring, for free, to help make your company successful. What should you be looking for? First and foremost, look for people you trust, respect, and like working with. Life is too short to work with people you can't look in the eye or depend upon. Call other entrepreneurs who have received financing and ask what the working relationship is like. Ask the venture capitalist for references—but not until they say they are going to make you an offer!

Next, articulate the holes in you or your team's ability, and look for those talents in your investor. Do they have deep domain knowledge in the infrastructure you need to build? Do they have great contacts and resources for recruiting? Are they well connected in the biz dev world? Your investor is not taking the place of a full-time employee, so you can't count on them to do an ongoing job, but they can be called upon for ongoing help in opening doors, sorting out business models, and recruiting. Look for a skill set and track record that speaks to your specific needs.

Finally, look at the team behind the person. Is there a strong partnership with others who can and will be of help? For example, one partner in our firm, Rex Golding, was a top investment banker before joining us. He's proven critically valuable to all our companies as the file their S1s and negotiate with their bankers. Look for partnerships with strong operating experience in the ranks. And look for a great portfolio of investments. At SOFTBANK, we're significant investors in over 100 Internet companies, which gives us the ability to open doors for our investments all over the Internet map. The noise level is so high in these companies that it becomes a huge leg-up when the investor/board member who walks you in the door also happens to be a board member of the company you want to hook into. Our portfolio companies also share information and resources that can help them succeed. The "netbatsu," or affiliation of net companies, can be a very powerful thing to become a part of.

How important is the role VCs play with entrepreneurs?

The right VCs can be tremendously helpful, but they don't take the place of a great CEO or a great management team. We can't run your companies for you, even though we may act like we want to sometimes. You have to be the person who picks up the flag each day and carries it to the top of the hill. We can't create the passion or the culture for your firm. We likely aren't going to be the one who jumps the red-eye to save the big customer order. That would be you, too. I was a CEO for almost 15 years before becoming a venture capitalist, and it is still sometimes hard for me to say, 'Well, here's what I would do, but it's up to you.' But it is, and the best VCs know where to draw that line.

Ultimately, it's your baby, and its success or failure rests largely on your shoulders. At best, your venture capitalist can be a trusted advisor, a shoulder to cry on, a dose of tough love at the right time, a powerful ally in the business development world, a closer for the employees you need, a cheerleader to the press, a powerful rolodex, and a strong mind to apply to the challenges you face. At worst, your venture capitalist can be just another problem for you to face each day. The greatest CEOs make their companies successful regardless of (or in spite of) their venture capitalists. But if you can choose, why not choose one that helps instead of hinders?

JAN HENRIC BUETTNER
Bertelsmann Ventures

Jan Henric Buettner is the founding General Partner of Bertelsmann Ventures (BV), the independent venture capital fund of one of the world's largest media companies, Bertelsmann AG. BV began its operations in 1998 as a private VC Limited Partnership with offices in New York and Santa Barbara, CA. After being deeply involved with the licensing for the GSM digital mobile network in Germany in the late Eighties, Jan and his team created one of the world's first multimedia online services in 1992. By 1994, Jan founded AOL Europe as a Joint Venture between America Online and Bertelsmann and became CEO of AOL Germany.

Bertelsmann Ventures has invested in companies such as ants.com, beMANY!, BeSonic.com, DealPilot.com, Done.com, ExpertCity.com, eGroups.com, imandi.com, MyZack.com, NuvoMedia, ONElist.com, and Riffage.com

How much of your fund is based on opportunities outside of the United States? What are some of the opportunities in the Internet space that you like right now?

Our first fund was mainly focused on opportunities on the West Coast. We are just closing our second fund that will be significantly larger and continue to focus on investments in the U.S. In addition, we will expand our activities into the European market, which is home territory for us. As the European Internet and capital markets are quickly catching up with the U.S., we will have a very strong presence there, especially in Germany. In total, I assume that our new fund will have a 50/50 split of invested capital between Europe and the US. On an investment level, we are traditionally very strong in the consumer market, where we currently see a shift away from the business-to-consumer approach. Our direction here continues to be towards consumer-to-consumer or even consumer-to-business opportunities. Examples of this trend can be seen by our investments in imandi.com (reverse marketplace) and beMANY! (buying club). In addition, we are very interested in the wireless space and are also looking for appealing business-to-business opportunities.

How much are you encouraging your portfolio companies to expand internationally?

One of our core competencies is the international approach. Through our networks in Europe and the U.S., we are actively helping our companies to establish a presence on the other side of the Atlantic once they are ready for this move. We do encourage the management teams to first build a successful and scalable business in their own geographical market and then to develop an aggressive internal international strategy.

What are the specific opportunities that you are looking to get involved in right now?

Right now, we are building our European presence, especially in Germany, France, and the UK. We are also looking for opportunities in the Scandinavian market, where the most innovative wireless services are being developed. In the U.S., we are currently looking to get involved in the entertainment market, as broadband becomes increasingly available.

Do you think the opportunities right now are better internationally than they are in the US?

I do not think they are better, but they are different. The development of the Internet market in the U.S. is far from being completed which continues to generate interesting investment opportunities. In Europe, a lot of Internet companies recently replicated successful U.S. businesses. In addition, we now see more and more original concepts being developed in Europe which then may be brought to the U.S. market as well. Our fund will be very active in both markets and will coordinate international relationships across the Atlantic.

Which industries do you feel are going to be the most affected over the next couple of years?

The Internet is affecting every industry. Generally, the power is being shifted away from big corporations towards networks and individuals, who will more and more get their fair share of the value created. Specifically, I see the media, telecommunications, and financial industry being mostly affected by this trend.

How much of a convergence do you think we are going to see between old world companies like Time Warner and new world companies like AOL?

Total convergence. The trend is to fully integrate dot com traffic and real world assets. Creating a new Internet brand today can cost close to $100 million, which makes it very attractive for new Internet startups to team up with brick and mortar businesses. But initiatives for this kind of cooperation do not only come from the "new economy." More and more managers of the "old economy" are very excited about finding ways to participate in the creation of new paradigms within their established industry.

How do your early stage companies look to create value?

The metrics that measure success of a startup company are changing over time. At one point, the emphasis was solely on customer attention or page views. Now we see a shift back to revenue and profit. In addition, focusing on customer satisfaction and quality can create value. We are encouraging our companies to create as much convenience and savings for the customer as possible - this will ultimately lead to the right mix of value generating success metrics.

What is it that you are looking for in the companies you invest in?

As we are mainly investing in early stage companies, our focus is on teaming up with the right people. We are a hands-on venture fund with deep strategic and operational industry knowledge, and we are actively helping our entrepreneurs to achieve their goals. Ideally, we are looking for an exciting and scalable business concept that is being implemented by an excellent management team.

Take me through the lifecycle of one of your portfolio companies.

A good example is eGroups, which is just going public this summer. We had identified the online community space as an area we wanted to be involved in, when we worked with ICQ in 1997. One year later, we became interested in eGroups, which was just looking for a first round of financing. After a very competitive situation on the term sheet level we decided to team up with another startup. Together with CMGI, we founded the company ONElist, which already had comparable metrics to eGroups. We helped ONElist to rapidly build their business in the U.S. and in Europe, hired their CEO, and when ONElist got ahead of eGroups in terms of traffic and users, we approached eGroups to merge the two companies. Our ONElist CEO quickly and successfully executed the merger as well as a second round of financing and now is the CEO of the combined entity. The renamed company became eGroups and is now is the dominant market leader in the group communication space.

How different is it to start an Internet or technology business in a different country than the U.S.?

Every market is different, especially because of different cultural backgrounds of the people involved. In Germany, for example, people are generally more risk averse than in the U.S., which has to be reflected by appropriate compensation packages and different equity participation. In the consumer marketplace, the success formula for a specific business varies a lot from country to country, even within Europe.

What are some of the biggest challenges you find your early stage companies having?

The biggest challenge is in execution. Entrepreneurs who start their first business always underestimate the difficulty in executing on their strategy. This is an area where we can add a lot of value in addition to helping the company find their place in various important business communities.

What are the key developments you feel will a major impact on the Internet economy?

In the near term, we are expecting the most important and exciting developments in services connected with the wireless and broadband markets. However, we are open for all kinds of revolutionary new business approaches and we even created our own software tools that help us identify trends very early on. We consider ourselves to be more like a high tech weapon that is prepared to look and aim at interesting new targets rather than having the targets identified right away. Once we have identified the right target, we know how to hit them.

What effect do you think a crash in the U.S. markets would have on the rate of new international ventures being started?

It would depend on the type of crash. We do not expect a general crash of the Internet market, but rather strong declines in certain sub-markets or on a company-by-company basis. The Internet is creating such dramatic changes for all industries, so that even very high valuations of certain companies, which reflect those future opportunities, are justifiable. However, if any of these companies or industry segments does not fulfill on the expectations of the investors, we will see dramatic cutbacks in valuations. On this end, Internet companies, which are already public, will be increasingly pushed towards meeting traditional comparables like revenue and profit. On the other end, we will continue to see excitement and high valuations for first movers and leaders of new market segments.

How are valuations of companies different in the U.S. versus other countries?

A. Valuations are a function of supply (of exciting new startups) and demand (amount of venture capital available). The most important issue that had to be solved in order to get more money into the European VC market was to create exit mechanisms similar to NASDAQ in the U.S. As this has been solved, we see valuations in Europe sometimes being even higher than in the US.

What should entrepreneurs be looking for in their funding sources?

They should look for an alignment of interest with the people they want to team up with. We look for trustworthy and performance driven entrepreneurs that have an exciting vision and the stamina to execute on it, even when times get tough. In return, we provide them with the experience, resources, networks, and visions required to turn groundbreaking ideas and business models into successful long lasting companies. It is like a marriage, you are teaming up for both the good and the bad times.

ALEX WILMERDING
Boston Capital Ventures

Alex Wilmerding has seven years of business development and operations management experience in the transportation industry. Alex managed business and operations projects in Shanghai, People's Republic of China, and Southeast Asia for Fednav Limited, after earning an MBA in Finance and Organizational Management at the Columbia Business School.

Boston Capital Ventures partnerships have invested in companies such as Advertising Communications International, Centric Software, Exa, JuniorNet, Revelation Technologies, Brooks Fiber Properties, ConXus Communications, Mediacom, MGC Communications, Powerfone/Nextel Communications, SCC Communications, Teletrac, 21st Century Telecom Group, UniSite, Verio, BrandDirect Marketing, Bright Horizons Child Care Centers, Conservation Tourism, The International Cornerstone Group, Intellon, Vectrix, Vertex Technologies, ILEX Oncology, MedSpan, Omnia, Parexel International, and Sensitech.

Tell me a little bit about the investment philosophy of your firm.

We have a focus on IT and communication services companies. An analogy we like to use is that we don't dig for gold, we like to fund the companies that are selling the shovels to the gold miners. So the focus is really on companies that have a 20 to 50 percent service component to their business and have some proprietary software or technology product or solution. We also look for products that can be customized with a service offering, which ultimately allows for an ongoing relationship with the customers and recurring revenue through a licensing relationship.

How important is it for a company to have proprietary technology?

The proprietary nature is important in that it should represent a significant differentiator and lead in the marketplace. Even if you wind up buying or licensing proprietary technology from someone else, you still need a significant lead in the marketplace, and I think that a company cannot just be a pure service organization. It has to be a company that's developed a solution that is germane to its success and which is not easily replicable within 12 to 18 months.

How far along does an entrepreneur or management team have to be in their venture for you to consider funding them?

The earliest stage at which we will fund a company is when they have an alpha or beta version of their "solution." The product or service can still be in trial, and they do not need to have any customers as of yet, but they need to at least have something that we can see. We need to know that the solution is very well aligned with a core of customers in their vertical market or in a specific segment of the market; it also needs to address a significant problem. It could even be that a company's been around for four or five years and has revenues—even $2 million in revenues—but has developed a standardized solution for the first time.

Where do you find that a lot of your focus is right now in terms of segments in the industry? Are you seeing a lot of business-to-business deals? Are you seeing a lot of opportunities in the e-commerce or broadband industries?

With the exception of one investment in BCV IV, most of our investments have been in the business-to-business space. And in terms of verticals, the only area in which we really have precluded ourselves from participating in is the health care and biotech industry. We just do not have the depth of experience in that area. But we'll still do a deal that will serve the technical side of these industries. Our drive here is very operating-focused, because we all have front-line operating experience from companies we had worked at previously. What we try to do is syndicate our knowledge with at least one other complementary partner who may have more vertical-related experience. For example, we just invested in a company called Veridium that helps organizations with large marketing and advertising budgets analyze return on investment through distribution channels. We have a lot of marketing and sales experience in this area, so what we've done is support the entrepreneur in bringing in other investors who have deep relationships in other core competency areas.

Besides the actual capital, what sort of intangibles do you bring to the table?

All of the entrepreneurs with whom we work seriously appreciate that we understand which models do and don't work in developing a service-oriented organization. They have a great deal of respect for our understanding of the models that will ultimately drive a company to success. I think that is what makes most of our relationships compelling and contributes to the value-added aspect. For companies that are just at an inflection point in their growth, it is critical that a company's sales and marketing strategies are structured in a way that is compelling for customers in need of a solution. BCV specializes in providing an appropriate level of guidance to entrepreneurs with whom we are able to establish good chemistry. After that is in motion, we also provide some of the more sophisticated M&A pieces of guidance, or bring in another partner from a complimentary firm which might, for example, have relevant M&A experience in a specific vertical.

How often do you see the sales and marketing strategy change throughout the course of their early-stage growth after you have worked with management to get a clear vision?

I think what's most important is that the sales and marketing strategy is crystallized by the time we make a commitment to invest in a firm or very soon thereafter. It should not change too much after that because we're looking for an 18 month window of very rapid sales growth. The assumption is that the solution should already be in line with the needs of a significant majority of customers in a vertical, and that the sales proposition clearly articulates how the product or service addresses a problem for these customers. If the marketplace *does* change and requires an offering change as well, it then becomes an issue of working among stakeholders to make sure that there's enough support for what really needs to happen. What we find that normally happens, however, is that when we work with companies very proactively— sometimes even before we end up funding them—that during this period that we are able to provide guidance as to the nature of an offering. I often visit with companies that might be three or four months from reaching a stage of development at which we would ordinarily invest, but part of the understanding is that we're spending time working together to do certain things. When they have improved their model or met certain parameters, both the entrepreneur and BCV will be ready to make a commitment to one another

What are those parameters that they need to meet? What are the milestones?

Let me talk about how we define the alpha or beta stage at which we like to invest. If a company has been a service organization, it is when the company has finally starting to "productize" a technology that we may be ready to make an investment. We need to see at least one solution that has been developed and see it in trial with a customer. It is also important to ensure the organization has the appropriate depth of people who have deep industry experience in a vertical in which the organization is going after. We also want to make sure that the company can provide an appropriate level of analytical and consulting guidance for a vertical-oriented solution and provide an IT integration capability that can allow a closer, more symbiotic relationship with customers.

What are some of the tangibles and the intangibles that greatly affect the valuation for the company?

The biggest tangibles are the existing satisfied customers, the money that's gone into the company to date, and the attendant expectations of current stakeholders. The companies that we invest in are not usually at the seed or development stage; they're at the expansion stage. If we're lucky enough to be in a situation where it's really been more friends and family investors to date, the understanding should be that there is room for future growth in valuation and incentives to management to really grow the company from a more modest valuation to one of significant value for both management and investors. If there's been another institutional round prior to our coming in, discussions about valuation and incentives for management are centered around previous benchmarks in this area. So our assessment of valuation is actually more dictated by what would we expect to see in the future for the company rather than on the past. We assume that 80 percent of our companies are going to be sold or entertain an acquisition strategy rather than look solely for internal organic growth and an IPO. So it's really the end game that will dictate some sort of discount on a future valuation. If we have confidence in where the company is and have spent time really working through their business model, from our perspective, there's enough comfort so that we're able to come up with a valuation that both parties will be happy with.

Let's say you're the first institutional round in the deal. How much capital should the entrepreneur be raising? Should they raise enough capital for a year or to get to a certain milestone?

There is no hard-and-fast rule, but I would say that the companies in which we're investing are at a distinct advantage because they're generally able to develop their service while still selling it to customers. So we're not funding companies that are spending two years developing a product and which cannot allocate a lot of R&D effectively to their customers. The stage at which we're investing is often one at which the funding is more ramp-up and expansion funding. The reason being is that if it came to a point where the subsequent funding wasn't available, the company could just cut back on some of its sales efforts and not expand as quickly. What we think entrepreneurs should look for is at least a year's worth of capital. We don't like to start working on another round at the same time that we close a current round of investment. That's why we're very averse to participating in companies that require majority of funding just for marketing. This tends to be a very binary sort of relationship. After six months, if the campaign hasn't worked, you're back to the drawing board with very little to show for the capital lost—except for possibly brand awareness. Companies that we're backing tend to have a solution that addresses a significant problem for another company—significant enough that there will be ongoing consulting and services revenue as well as licensing revenue.

Are you encouraging your portfolio companies to take on some sort of bank debt from a venture bank?

We encourage leasing obligations, and there are some very good firms who specialize in that. We otherwise don't encourage a great deal of leverage, the reason being that we prefer to keep that in our back pocket for the company later down the road when receivables financing may become necessary.

Tell me about a couple of Internet or technology businesses that you think will end up being the most profitable in the long run.

I have two very good examples, one of which is a company called EXA Corporation. EXA has developed a software solution utilizing Digital Physics to solve the problem of fluid flow analysis for computerized applications in the automotive, aerospace, and chemical process industries. Its solutions allow companies to save hundreds of thousands of dollars by creating cost-efficient alternatives to traditional modeling, including use of wind tunnels. EXA allows you to analyze engine blocks and determine where hot spots are, in addition to modeling the movement of currents within petroleum and other sorts of equipment. It allows an organization—like Chrysler or any of the other top automotive companies—to figure out how to quickly remove an obstacle or create an opportunity in a process that has traditionally been fundamentally very costly and very slow.

Similarly, we have invested in a company called Centric Software that provides a digital manufacturing platform that allows an entire organization—be it Boeing or Volvo—to model the development of a product and to share changes across an entire organization. It also allows a very vibrant simulation environment where individuals can plug and play different components and understand some of the parameters that are involved in adding and subtracting different parts. Solutions like these that engage a consultancy services piece as part of the offering and have a very proprietary platform are able to crush the traditional perception of a development cycle and develop a long-standing relationship with their customers. We've done some very clear infrastructure plays; however, the direction in which we're moving now is figuring out how to support some of these industries through the solutions I've been describing. We have great respect for some of the business to the consumer dot coms of the world, but ultimately we feel the opportunities which are most significant are those which are business-to-business solutions.

What types of industries do you feel are still going to be affected the most by the Internet?

Any manufacturing industry. Basically, it will be any organization that has global procurement processes or a global network of offices or of services. I cannot think of a company that's ultimately not going to be affected by the Internet.

The market's been bullish for so long and obviously a lot of venture capital is driven by the private equity markets and that liquidity feature. What are some of the key indicators that you watch for in terms of the Internet economy changing?

We look at the types of deals that are coming to us as a way of gauging how entrepreneurs are changing their approach as well as how the market is moving them to change their approach. What we are looking for in terms of signals are opportunities or trouble signs in M&A activity in certain verticals. Certain segments are clearly becoming more prone to opportunities for entrepreneurs because of the M&A activity within that industry. The second thing we look for is specialization. The more developed sectors are starting to encourage entrepreneurs to focus on very specialized products and services. This confirms to us that those areas are becoming much more capital-intensive and competitive, and over time are much more likely to require a lot of M&A expertise. Ultimately, the most important way to stay on top of things is by noticing subtle changes in the marketplace.

We're obviously hearing so much from a technology and Internet standpoint about what's happening

overseas. Is there a rush for your portfolio companies to expand internationally?

I would say that the temptation is very real. I say "temptation" because the business models that we're backing don't necessarily require immediate expansion overseas. We believe that their strength is in improving themselves domestically, and that there's a place internationally and great opportunity to move business models abroad at a specific point in time. I worked in Asia for about seven years and have a very deep understanding of how that region and its economy work. But all of our companies have great opportunities here and, if anything, expanding internationally right now is sometimes a distraction because it involves trying to move into several markets concurrently. There's great second-stage growth opportunity abroad, but we're not looking for them to rush into foreign markets immediately.

What do you think are some of the greatest financial hurdles that a company has when they're first starting?

The biggest financial hurdle is developing the right sales and pricing strategies from the beginning. Especially when you are a new company and you want to cut a deal to get two or three reference clients, the temptation to bend on prices is very significant. You don't, however, want those relationships to dilute your opportunity for truly leveraging the economic value of your solution with future clients. If anything, it's being able to be disciplined enough and impressive enough to prove to your customer that your value is as high as you believe it to be.

At what point should a company actually have a CFO? Should they have one in place from the beginning or should they wait for a later stage?

I think there's always going to have to be someone who takes on the role of financial director, you may just not call him or her a CFO initially. But in today's market, that may mean someone who's bright and has a business school degree, but not necessarily someone who came out of a big-five accounting firm and has depth of CFO experience. I don't think it's always requisite for us at the first stage of expansion, but very quickly the skills of a sophisticated CFO are required.

When you have an investment that isn't going the way it was supposed to, what are the indicators that tell you it's time to stop funding the company?

It's time to stop funding the company when you're six months beyond really being able to help them. When we have a board role, we expect to have board meetings probably once every six weeks to two months, or to at least have conversations with the CEO on a weekly or bi-weekly basis. So we tend to have a close enough relationship with the company that we can tell when reference accounts are not coming in and if there's a problem. If we have been misled, those assumptions will probably be revealed to us far too late in the game to make any change. So we'd like to think that when we have a board role, we're more likely to be able to anticipate issues and work them through before curtailing funding is an issue. However, I think the trouble signs are probably there some six months in advance. It's only when you cannot find a way of encouraging all the stakeholders to work toward a logical course of resolution that it may end up leading to liquidation or a closure of the company. I think the bottom line is being able to anticipate the problems, having the ability to stay on top of your relationships with your investors, and making sure that you're always accessible.

ANDREW FILIPOWSKI
divine interVentures

Andrew "Flip" Filipowski is one of the world's most successful high-tech entrepreneurs, philanthropists, and industry visionaries. He built one of the top 10 global software companies in record time and now devotes all of his expertise, thought, leadership, and entrepreneurial talent to his company divine interVentures. Founded by Flip in 1999, divine is an Internet operating company actively engaged in business-to-business e-commerce through a network of partner companies. divine's Internet Zaibatsu™ family of companies collaborates to create success through a tightly linked network. divine acquires significant interests in, operates, and provides services to its partner companies.

Flip founded PLATINUM technology International, inc. in 1987 and served as the chairman of the board, president, and chief executive officer until its sale in 1999 to Computer Associates. PLATINUM technology provided infrastructure management software and services to the top 10,000 information technology users in the world, helping CIOs minimize the risk of enterprise computing. Its sale went into the record books as the single largest software transaction in history for more than $3.6 billion.

divine interVentures' Internet Zaibatsu family encompasses companies such as aluminum.com, beautyjungle.com, bid4real.com, bidbuybuild, Buzz divine, CapacityWeb.com, closerlook, Commerx, Community divine, comScore, divine interchange, dotspot divine, eFiltration.com, e-Reliable Commerce, eXperience divine, Farms.com, FiNetrics, Host divine, I-Fulfillment, iGive, iSalvage.com, I-Street, Justice divine, Knowledge divine, LAUNCHworks, LiveOnTheNet, Martin Partners, Mercantec, mindwrap, Neoforma, NTE, OfficePlanIt.com, OilSpot, OpinionWare, Outtask, Perceptual Robotics, PocketCard, Sales divine, Sequoia Software, sho research, Talent divine, TheExecClub, TV House, ViaChange.com, Web Design Group, Westbound Consulting, Whiplash, Xippix, and Xqsite.

You grew PLATINUM *technology* from startup into one of the largest and most successful software companies ever. Why did you then decide to sell the company to Computer Associates?

Up until the moment that I met with Sanjay Kumar on the evening of March 22nd, 1999, the company was not for sale—and was not for sale under any circumstance to Computer Associates. Every plan and every action we took was to maintain an independent company. Even that evening, the entire purpose was to make sure CA got the message that PLATINUM was not for sale. It was only after hearing the offer that I felt I had no choice but to execute my fiduciary responsibility and present—and then support—the offer for the benefit of our shareholders. It was neither my choice nor my decision; it was my *responsibility* at that point that led to the announced sales on March 29th, 1999. In retrospect, PLATINUM's success bred a certain amount of discontent. The sale of the company to Computer Associates turned out to be a liberating event: It allowed us to launch a company like divine interVentures.

What drove you to build another company after PLATINUM *technology*?

I don't know of any other activity that could fill my time so enjoyably between now and death. Deep in my person, I believe that entrepreneurship is the greatest form of philanthropy. I find most other activities to be far less stimulating and far less personally rewarding than conquering the fear that comes with creating a business. With divine interVentures we have an opportunity to build a company that will create tremendous value and may help re-define the very essence of what a corporation will look like in the future. The Internet is an inflection point that rivals and perhaps overshadows some of the greatest inflection points of our time—the automobile, electricity, the telephone, railroads, television. But all of those inflection points were catalysts for even greater social changes. It wasn't just the automobile, but the highway network built to support the automobile that changed society. The Internet and the resulting network have the same social implications. Organizations from the last century (that do not have the ability to adapt) will not survive into the next. Corporations and partnership structures will need to change dramatically to adapt to the employees, investors, and customers of this new era. Discovering and creating these new organizational structures is a great and exciting high-stakes chess game.

Plus, there's no greater waste in the world than having an entrepreneur retire.

Tell me about your company, divine interVentures.

The digital economy is revving up here in the heartland, and we think divine interVentures is one of the catalysts of this growth. We are a Chicago-based operating company engaged in business-to-business Internet commerce. We're building a closely-knit network of partner companies by securing significant interest in and operating a broad range of e-commerce companies and integrating them into the Internet Zaibatsu™. At divine interVentures, we empower the companies within the Internet Zaibatsu to overcome rapidly changing market conditions and stay ahead of the curve by offering all of the necessary business components: managerial expertise, operating services, networking resources, incubation space, and industry knowledge. Our solutions shorten our partners' time to market or to execute an IPO and also foster post-IPO growth in an evolving market.

From an organizational standpoint, how is divine interVentures different than PLATINUM *technology*?

PLATINUM *technology* was a great company, but it was based on an outdated business model. Companies that insist upon embracing this model will begin to perish. That process has already begun. When I was growing up in the fifties, employees expected companies to exist longer than the employees themselves. Recently, however, the half-life of companies has significantly diminished. They're born, enter mid-life and then die within our own lifetime. divine interVentures is our interpretation of the next generation of companies that will dominate in the decades ahead.

What do you mean by Internet Zaibatsu?

divine interVentures is the Internet Zaibatsu. A zaibatsu is a Japanese concept, describing a group of interrelated businesses that work collaboratively to create mutual opportunity. What differentiates a zaibatsu is that it has a leadership model. That is missing from today's keiretsus in Japan. It is a term borrowed from the past. We are, in fact, an economic coalition of companies.

What is the difference between a zaibatsu and a keiretsu?

The keiretsu model is based on consensus, and can confound itself with painfully slow decision-making processes. Zaibatsu refers to traditional Japanese, family-owned conglomerates, which were extremely successful until they were banned following World War II.

How does the zaibatsu model apply to divine interVentures?

divine interVentures is a community or family of Internet businesses composed of service providers, partner companies, and strategic associates. Our goal is to create resilient Internet businesses for the New Economy. It will be increasingly difficult for companies to operate outside of this model. By the end of this century, I expect most companies in the S&P 100 to be based on this model. We believe strongly that the zaibatsu model transcends the traditional venture capital model in sustaining beneficial partnerships because it enables entrepreneurs to focus on their core business while we provide the operational services they need to be aggressive competitors in a market that is evolving at Internet-speed. The new economy is not about technology; it's about collaboration and bridging all constituents to the next universal form of business—the Internet. Our goal is to build a thriving Internet economy in the Midwest region, where businesses can leverage the wealth of opportunity and established business-to-business industry expertise, whether it be manufacturing, travel, or agriculture. It's not e-commerce—it's *the* commerce.

How do next-generation companies like divine interVentures differ from today's successful companies?

Traditional companies contain the seeds of their own demise. They are not structured for the accelerated pace demanded by the New Economy. The enterprises that will survive and excel will be conglomerates whose "member companies" share a common vision and can leverage collective strengths. They will be economic coalitions, or e-coalitions.

Why did some of the conglomerates of the past not succeed?

The model for the conglomerates of the past was a failure because it was based on a centralized management structure that squelched the entrepreneurial spirit and resulted in organizational sclerosis. Our vision at divine interVentures borrows from some leading organizational experiments of the past—like the Berkshire Hathaway model, or Thermal Electron, and certainly from contemporaries like CMGI. We're not out to completely own and rigorously control all of the companies under our aegis. We provide new ventures with a corporate home, but allow them to retain significant ownership and make their own business decisions. We strongly believe that the essence of an organization is that it is an atomic unit—not a subatomic unit incapable of standing alone but a real business doing one thing very well. If it begins doing more than one thing, it should break apart into its atomic units. These units then continue with common management, common board members, and cooperate through partial ownership of each other and belong to an Ecolition that in turn can be owned by a higher-level Ecolition. This allows employees to work for an atomic unit and maximize their work in the creation of shareholder value. They are isolated to some degree from the other units and do not suffer if other units stumble, but are measured by shareholders as stand-alone entities. Investors prefer—and generally assign far greater value to—collections of atomic units than they do conglomerates. To succeed in the future, current homogenous organizations like GE will potentially break apart into their atomic units, cooperate at the Ecolition level, and attain even greater value in the aggregate then they do now.

eBrandedBooks.com
Get Published!

Is divine interVentures an incubator?

We accidentally get lumped into the incubator grouping because it is a popular category and analysts and the press like simple descriptions. The descriptive terms for our kind of organizations haven't been agreed to yet, so until terms like Ecolition are adopted, others will try to lump us into convenient pigeonholes. It's a little like when we called an automobile a horse-less carriage. Divine interVentures represents a far broader strategy than incubators and venture capital firms.

Tell me about your team at divine interVentures.

The divine interVentures team includes Mike Cullinane, former CFO of PLATINUM technology and current CFO for divine; Paul Humenansky, former COO of PLATINUM and president of Business Development for divine; and Scott Hartkopf, a seasoned professional with impressive operational expertise, who joins divine as president and COO. We're also proud to employ a wealth of experienced professionals in the key operational areas in which our partner companies require strategic guidance and support, including marketing, human resources, accounting, IT hosting, web design, and development, legal and other areas. These tremendously successful executives have— among their combined achievements—built worldwide sales forces, established a global network of offices, managed corporate real estate and facilities, built and managed a global computing and telecommunications network, provided corporate legal counsel and run highly profitable businesses. I could not be more proud or excited about the divine interVentures team.

What role does divine interVentures' management play in the e-coalition?

We seek to keep all of our companies focused on a common goal: To create tremendously unfair advantages over the competition. In some ways we also serve a role that could be described as similar to a film producer. With the half-life of companies getting shorter, it becomes important to more fully develop companies in a shorter period of time. We can bring to the table all the components that complement an entrepreneurial effort rather quickly, thereby cutting the gestation period to just a fraction of the time that it would normally take.

How do you create unfair advantages over the competition?

We create these advantages in three ways. First, we're focused on Internet companies that have the mindset to put every other competitor in their industry out of business—we're looking for the big, aggressive idea. Companies that just want to generate earnings by being number two or three in their market are not a fit for us. Second, we provide a service menu to Internet companies. We provide a wide array of essential business services, including web design, hosting, legal counsel, public relations and marketing, office facilities, recruiting and benefits services, accounting and financial services, as well as our own experience in building dot coms. We want the entrepreneurs to focus solely on creating value by penetrating the market with the right products and services. Third, all of the companies associated with divine interVentures have an Internet infrastructure or business-to-business focus, and each can benefit from relationships with the other companies. Our management team is constantly seeking to identify mutually beneficial opportunities among our various companies. This allows the sum of the parts to be far greater than the whole, and that can create huge competitive advantages. This is the power of the Internet Zaibatsu family.

Are the companies within the Internet Zaibatsu required to use these services?

No. That was the idea with the old conglomerate model, where centralized management wanted to put its hands into everything. We do not do that. If one of our companies within the Internet Zaibatsu believes it has great public relations capabilities or can do great web development, then they may have a strong argument to proceed by themselves. However, it's very clear that the availability of all of these services within the Internet Zaibatsu can provide our companies with a significant advantage over competitors who have to fend for themselves.

How did you come up with the zaibatsu model for divine interVentures?

I saw the need to re-invent the corporation in order to align it with the realities of the New Economy. I looked at business models all over the world, and it became clear that a new model would have to address the accelerated pace of the New Economy. Many great ideas are germinated in startups, rather than in the bowels of large corporate structures. I also saw a need to get away from consensus management. My research led me to the zaibatsu, which possessed many of the attributes I was interested in—especially the ability to create competitive advantages through collective action.

Where did the name divine interVentures come from?

We originally thought we would be called Sticky Angels but it didn't stick. Then one day we were having lunch with a few of the folks and one our execs, Mike Santer, said, "You know, we're sort of trying to be a divine intervention in the high-tech community by providing them with all of the different things they may need." We ran with that idea and came up with the current variant.

Why is divine interVentures focused on Internet companies?

We don't perceive ourselves to be as much Internet-focused as we are focused on companies that are exploiting technology to redefine business. The ubiquity and efficiency of the Internet lends itself to be exploited by the zaibatsu. We're actually aggregation-focused: Every company we select has to have a reason to exist within the Internet Zaibatsu. It is through this consolidated effort that we hope to create massively unfair advantages for our companies.

Why is divine interVentures focused on Internet companies in the Midwest?

We are actually focused on under-served areas across the globe. Right now, the wealth created by the New Economy is actually aggregated in just a few places; the rest of the country is left out. Dot com startups in the Midwest have a tremendous wealth of talent to draw upon, both inside and outside our great universities. Dot com startups and infrastructure companies in particular will flourish in the Midwest with sufficient financing opportunities and other types of key support. In addition to our headquarters in Chicago, we recently opened up our presence in Austin, Calgary, and Israel, and we have still more plans to open other centers across the globe.

What are the ingredients needed to recreate Silicon Valley in the Chicago land area?

Having been in the Chicago technology market for many years, I have seen the vast potential of this area. We are on the cusp of fulfilling that potential. We have all of the necessary components as a community to make this ambitious goal a reality. Already in place are many great ideas, willing entrepreneurs, and programs that the Mayor of Chicago and the Governor of Illinois have spearheaded to ensure we build a strong Internet economy. Chicago is poised to become a leading Internet economy—we certainly have momentum. The Milken Institute, for example, recently raised Chicago's ranking among technologically influential cities from 20 to eight, and from there we will quickly move into the top three. We are the fourth-largest region in the country in high-tech industry employment and headquarter more than 8,000 technology-based businesses. We have the world's premier business and technology educational institutions, including University of Illinois, University of Chicago, Northwestern, and the Illinois Institute of Technology. Our city leadership and community are working together with divine interVentures to build the top Internet businesses, which will ensure that Chicago has all of the necessary components to achieve this goal. divine has received hundreds upon hundreds of calls in the last several months from companies that have heard about our plans and are interested in becoming a partner in the Internet Zaibatsu. We have also received numerous calls from businesses in the Bay area, Boston, and New York who want to align with us. We may see many businesses relocate to Chicago to be a part of this exciting economy.

Why are such high-profile people like the Mayor of Chicago and Governor of Illinois showing strong support for divine interVentures?

Although the Midwest hasn't suffered from a recession in a long time, its traditional industrial base is vulnerable. The state and local governments understand that building a digital economy will provide the region with a lot more diversification to help weather the inevitable down periods of the future.

How important is scale? When do you reach critical mass?

This is not an issue in the foreseeable future. There are a multitude of opportunities available and an infinite amount of funding, programs, and support to develop this market for a significant number of years. Looking at Silicon Valley, it is clear that growth and potential have been sustained, which means a healthy, expansive, abundant market for Chicago and other regions as well.

Are there specific virtues or characteristics of the region that might impede or foster its success?

Chicago is a great city in the center of everything with many strengths and virtues. We have strong leadership, tremendous talent, access to great educational institutions, a balanced economy, a strong workforce, and a powerful work ethic. It is a city of diversity and opportunity. The passion to build this economy is tremendous, the team effort unparalleled. At one time, Chicago was nearly wiped out by a fire. But the city, armed with a plan, rebuilt Chicago into what it is today—a leading center for commerce, culture, education, and architecture, not to mention one of the most beautiful cities in the world. We have before us an opportunity to create something great that will profoundly change our lives.

How do you plan for your new enterprise to integrate with other aspects of the region—say, the academic community?

This is the power of the Internet Zaibatsu. As part of the divine interVentures family, our partner companies will be able to leverage the relationships and resources that each of them has and that divine interVentures provides. Within the Internet Zaibatsu, we will have leaders from all key aspects of the regional environment, or will at least have close relationships with these leaders. Senior faculty members from both Kellogg and the University of Chicago sit on our board. For example, the divine interVentures management team is working directly with Chicago Mayor Richard Daley and his team on issues such as funding and office space for Chicago's Internet entrepreneurs. We have also begun work with Governor George Ryan. The divine interVentures management team has strong relationships with leaders in academia, traditional business, trade associations and other areas. As a part of the Internet Zaibatsu, companies will have fast and easy access to the relationships and resources they need to rapidly grow their businesses. We will work with the educational institutions to build internship programs and mentor entrepreneurial development. In addition to that, we have many philanthropic interests and responsibilities.

What's to prevent any other region from doing the same thing?

There is nothing to prevent it. In fact, we encourage it. The opportunities for companies like divine interVentures are so great that there is room for many more advocates. Consider a company with a business model comparable to ours—CMGI in Boston and Internet Capital Group in Wayne, Pennsylvania. CMGI and divine InterVentures recently formed a strategic relationship to benefit both companies' networks of Internet ventures. CMGI is also making a strategic investment in divine InterVentures. Internet Capital Group is represented on divine interVentures' board of directors. There is a tremendous need for regions outside of Silicon Valley to build Internet economies. Otherwise, we will only widen the gap between the haves and the have-nots—economically and socially. This is not good for anyone—not Silicon Valley, not Milwaukee, not anyone. It is not good to have so much wealth and opportunity centered around just certain areas.

Is your biggest concern that the Midwest will be slow in moving into the Internet economy?

If investment capital doesn't flow into the area. I know divine interVentures' capital will be there. But this undertaking isn't something just one company or one individual can accomplish. It's going to take the collective effort of the business community, the academic community, and the political community. It's going to take everyone. Certainly the corporate establishment in this area has to take a parental view as opposed to a self-centered view. I wonder if our corporate establishment will understand that they have to make room for and invest in the next generation of companies—regardless of whether they feel it is a natural process or not. The truth is that they're going to be affected that way. It's a very difficult ego thing to get accustomed to.

In many cities and regions, technology does not get as much attention from policymakers as do many other social and economic programs. How do you think this lack of attention to fostering tech economies will affect these cities and regions in the future?

Until policymakers view technology as a comprehensive growth tool that permeates every facet of society, business, politics, and education—rather than an industry in itself—technology may never be viewed with sufficient critical importance to help a city or region grow to its potential. What's even worse, the policymakers don't understand the peril under which our traditional business economy operates today.

Why do you say divine interVentures is not a venture capital firm?

divine interVentures is the antithesis of a venture capital firm. Venture capital firms finance startups with the idea of selling them in order to generate liquidity to make another investment: divine interVentures will never be a seller. Instead, we partially acquire leading edge companies that will dominate their market for the extent of their useful life—however long that may be. When a venture capital firm wants to sell the shares of one of our companies, we want to be the buyer.

What is your analysis of the state of the venture capital industry?

I think traditional venture capitalists in general are stuck in a business model that is obsolete. With any degree of self-analysis, the venture capitalists would find that they have created the ultimate non-scalable business, which is one of the criticisms that most venture capitalists levy on entrepreneurs. They themselves are the greatest victims. Therefore, whole new structures of the way businesses are created and innovation is fostered are going to come about as a result of the creation of e-coalitions, those economic coalitions between atomic companies and atomic organizations. These organizations are, in fact, going to take on a greater role, replacing and supplanting venture capital, and before the end of the next decade, they are going to replace venture capital and take on the responsibility of funding new businesses. My opinion is that the whole partnership structure—which involves venture capital firms, investment bankers, lawyers, and accountants—is an extinct model. It does not have all the components of value creation. It *can't* be evergreen; it will perish during the course of the next decade.

How much of a role in structuring the Internet economy have venture capitalists played?

The capital that has been provided—not only by venture capitalists, but also by various organizations that have invested, partnered, and supported Internet businesses— has, at a fundamental level, allowed the inflection point to blossom in a very short period of time. That has led to cultural changes, and a lot of that has been built on the availability of capital. Without that capital, some of these changes would have been a lot slower in coming forth, and the processes would be a lot more prone to error.

What is the investment philosophy of divine interVentures?

Our method of nurturing new businesses in a new cycle for new industries is to partner with those companies. Much in the same way a movie studio provides all of the talent necessary to produce a movie, we make it a far simpler process to launch and build an Internet business. In essence, we bring together a lot of the fundamental infrastructure items—not only the capital, but also things like accounting, finance, sales, and fundamental technologies. We provide an entire ecology for them to tap into, so it more closely resembles a movie production than it does a re-creation of the entire infrastructure in order to get a new business off the ground. An analogy I like to use is that most businesses today, when they're using venture capitalists, are in many ways like a movie studio that's reinventing the movie camera each time. Instead, we bring all the players to the table and assemble an atomic company out of the piece parts, many of which come from us.

How does the divine interVentures philosophy differ from that of venture capitalist firms?

We have a more permanent relationship—and contemplate a more permanent relationship—with our partners. We do not look forward to a point where we dispose of our investment. We look to grow with a company and build its value over an extended period of time.

Who are the big players in the Internet economy right now?

CMGI, Internet Capital Group, divine interVentures, idealab, and Kleiner Perkins.

What do you think are some of the best business opportunities that are waiting to be capitalized upon?

I think the best are those that will be built upon the human genome.

Do you have examples of what types of opportunities might come of that?

Gene therapy and the ability to analyze how one can extend human life with less debilitating disease.

What do you consider to be the best type of business model for an Internet company?

A company that does one atomic function and aims at a very large market where the atomic unit can generate billions of dollars in revenue.

What do you mean by "atomic?"

By "atomic" I mean a single, discreet, complete function.

Which Internet companies do you admire the most?

The Internet companies I admire most are Priceline, Neoforma, Bluestone, and eShare.

Is there a shared trait or characteristic that you find in each of them?

They share a very passionate focus on the atomic elements of their organizations.

How do you value an Internet business? What do you look at?

At divine interVentures, we look at the market opportunity, growth rate, and the ability to capture a dominant position in the space.

What are you specifically looking for when you make an investment? If a startup company comes to you, how do you analyze that company?

We look at the market and the ability of that company to excel within the market. But more important, we look at the people involved and whether or not they have the passion and ability to execute.

Who do you think are going to be the major players in e-commerce in five years?

I think a company that is a coalition of atomic units, an Ecolition.

So, for example, a company that has a model like divine interVentures or CMGI?

Correct. In fact, I expect that most companies in the Fortune 500 will have that model.

What effect do you think Internet companies are having on traditional brick-and-mortar companies?

Internet companies are replacing, supplementing, and absorbing traditional brick-and-mortar companies, thereby creating hybrid companies. As every business is transformed around the availability of certain technologies—such as the Internet, current industries and traditional business processes find themselves perilously close to obsolescence. Many businesses that are here today will not successfully cross the Internet chasm to participate in the next millennium as leaders in the new economy. They will more than likely remain and linger as they wither, becoming irrelevant to their communities, their shareholders—and unfortunately, to their employees.

What do you think brick-and-mortar companies must do to survive?

They must spin out companies that will replace them. Just like humans, businesses have to spawn their own children. The Chicago Tribune, for example, is spawning off news businesses while keeping its own core business relevant. A new kind of corporation is quickly emerging. It's a corporation that has elements in both investing and innovation, which helps create value at different levels, such as at the individual department level and at each individual portfolio business level. Each part has to have value and must be able to raise capital and motivate employees separately. The model is about partial acquisitions and ownerships that then form a whole. Companies have to steer all of their heart and soul in that direction. Some companies, like Charles Schwab and Dell Computers, have done it. But there are a thousand other companies out there that are not going to make the turn— they will fade away.

Do you think there are particular industries that are going to be affected more than others and need to act more quickly?

No, I think they are all in equal jeopardy. Tremendous economic change, of course, has happened before. Automobiles, for example, usurped the railroads as the main mode of transportation. Now it's the brick-and-mortar companies' turn to die. It will happen with the ubiquity of the Internet protocol. Most of the brick-and-mortar companies still look at the Internet as an add-on business—

that is, until they get a scare. Then they either change or die.

Just how significant are the changes that the Internet is having on our economy?

In a few years, we will not refer to "the Internet Economy." It will be just "the economy." Remember, we once received *mail*. Then we received *email*. Then we needed a term like *snail mail*. I assure you that when we say "mail" in the future, its first meaning will be what we call email today. First we had *commerce*, then *e-commerce*, so we had to come up with the term *brick-and-mortar* to define the commerce that pre-dated the Internet. Ultimately, what we know as e-commerce today will be the only commerce we know. This kind of technological transformation requires significant venture capital, human capital, and knowledge. Communities need to invest in the businesses that will replace the aging dinosaurs of our economic heritage. These new businesses will be the businesses that we will simply refer to as the banks, the insurance companies, the tourist attractions, and the schools of the future economy.

Does the traditional way of measuring a company's success—by earnings per share—still apply?

Measuring a company solely by earnings per share is naive. This obsession with earnings per share is the La Brea Tar Pits of the New Economy—it will trap many traditional corporations. A company must be measured by its contribution to society, market share, growth, innovation, cost to society, and—yes—by its ability to earn money.

How should companies be evaluated?

Ecolitions like divine interVentures need to be measured by how much value they create rather than by quarterly earnings, which are really more appropriate for measuring the individual atomic companies. This involves using a much more elaborate and less one-dimensional model to evaluate companies. It would include hundreds of different variables. It would ask, for example, what is a company's cost to society at large, to the community in which it resides, and to the environment? Or it would ask, how much does a company contribute to divine interVenture's goal of becoming a giant, highly efficient economic coalition?

What do you think is most exciting about being a part of the market to launch and foster Internet startups?

The ability to work with young entrepreneurs and entrepreneurs who are trying to establish new businesses, oftentimes creating very innovative new business cycles.

What do you mean by new business cycles?

Every time major inflection points—technological ones in particular—are introduced, a whole series of new businesses and new industries are born. And when you're at the leading edge of some of this, it's very exciting.

Considering your personal investments, what do you weigh most heavily when you invest in a venture outside of divine interVentures?

I look for how value can be built. That means looking at what customers want: if a certain venture serves the customer better than anyone else then, in most cases, that company will win. I also look for a management team that has an innovative approach to serving the customer. They should be willing to challenge the common thoughts and they should be willing to take risks. For example, when a company tells me that its customers want quality, I ask, "How do you know?" Sometimes the customer doesn't want quality, or has a different idea of what constitutes quality than the product or service provider.

How do you think you are viewed within the technology community?

I hope that, having built a billion-dollar software company, I represent a certain base of knowledge. I take pride in the fact that, to date, I have helped build two companies worth well over a billion dollars each. The first was Cullinet Corporation—the Microsoft of the 70s and 80s; the second was PLATINUM. I hope the third will be divine. I hope that I am a model to budding entrepreneurs, especially those in areas outside of Silicon Valley. I would like to think that I serve as a mentor. Working with other great entrepreneurs in this area, I hope to somehow contribute to this area gaining a significant foothold in the Internet economy.

How did your childhood influence the course you have set for yourself?

I grew up in an immigrant family who absolutely believed that our being in the US was a gift. We were poor, but I never knew want. My mother was a welder, my father a butcher. She helped get me a scholarship to a military school. At this school, it quickly became apparent to me that many of my wealthy classmates were not very motivated. I figured that if they could succeed in business, then there was no stopping anyone with the determination and passion to succeed.

SUZANNE KING
New Enterprise Associates

Suzanne King is a partner of NEA, focusing on information technology investments. Prior to joining NEA, Suzanne worked as Controller of XcelleNet, Inc. (now Sterling Commerce), a developer of system management software for remote access. She was part of XcelleNet's startup management team that grew the company to a successful IPO in 1994. Suzanne also worked as a senior auditor for Arthur Andersen & Co. where she specialized in small business and information technology.

NEA has invested in Internet and e-commerce companies such as UUNET Technologies, Be, Advertising.com, BeyondWork, BigOnline, BizTravel.com, Boxerjam, CareerBuilder, Convene.com, Cyveillance, eXcelon Corporation, iAsia Works, IndusRiver Networks, InSoft, Kana Communications, Macromedia, Netcentives, Packeteer, Sitara Networks, Telegea.com, Tripod, Applix, Clarify, CyberMedia, Epicor Software, iManage, Inso, Mission Critical Software, Mobius Management Software, ObjectShare, Progress Software, Software Publishing, 3Com, Bay Networks, Com21, Gadzoox Networks, Juniper Networks, Quantum Bridge Communications, Silicon Graphics, Adaptec, Cirrus Logic, QuickLogic, Vitesse Semiconductor, eBenefits, Echopass, eCommerce

Industries, Egreetings Network, E*Offering, EqualFooting.com, eTranslate, eZiba.com, FullAudio, Garageband.com, Home Account, HotDispatch, HydraWeb Technologies, Intarka, Loancity.com, Sierra Atlantic, SupplyBase, Technical Communities, and Xigo.

Tell me about the investment philosophy of NEA and how it is different from other venture capital firms.

Something that makes us different from a lot of other firms in this day and age is that we have been around for 22 years. We are in our ninth fund, have $2.6 billion under management, and just closed an $865 million fund in January. People think of us as a big, later stage fund, but we are actually early stage, first round investors. We are usually classified as the largest early-stage fund.

We generally invest in the first institutional round, usually Series A Preferred, and are very active by taking a board seat in about 80% of our investments. We also spend a lot of time recruiting executives, working on strategy, and introducing them to potential customers through our vast network. Another advantage is that we have invested in over 400 companies, about 128 of which have gone public and 134 that have been sold or merged. So we really have a big portfolio that we can pull resources from. A lot of our portfolio companies are actually customers of each other. For example, we were investors in both UUNet and Ascend; we introduced them to each other and UUNet became Ascend's biggest customer.

I think philosophically we are different in that we are incredibly supportive of our entrepreneurs through thick and thin. We think of ourselves as partners with the entrepreneurs, not just coming in with the money and bringing in our own management team. Our philosophy is that the entrepreneur should be the one in the limelight, not us.

Another thing that makes us unique is that as a partnership we compensate all our partners equally on every deal. Therefore, every partner is just as incentivized to do things for other partner's deals as they are their own. So I have partners on both coasts that do a lot of things for all of my companies. I think this speaks to our firm's philosophy in that we are very much a partnership. When entrepreneurs choose NEA as a partner, they are not just getting the point person, they are getting the whole network.

How do you invest in early-stage companies with such a large fund?

The reason we raised such a big fund is that companies today need more money than they used to. It used to be that you could put $5 to $7 million in a software company and that was all they needed before they went public. But in today's marketplace, time is everything and capital becomes a strategic advantage because it gets you there more quickly. Instead of being $2 or $3 million, first round investments are now $10 or $15 million. So in terms of the number of companies, we are investing in more, but they are also going out the other end more quickly in terms of going public or being sold. So it used to be that we would sit on boards for seven years, now it is maybe two to four years or even less. So in terms of the number of deals we are doing at any one time, we have still been able to keep that in the 10- to 12-company range for each individual partner.

What is it that catches your eye in the flurry of business plans that cross your desk?

Unless a deal comes in as a referral it really doesn't get a lot of attention. You have so many deals being referred by people that you respect that you need to at least look at. I would tell entrepreneurs the best thing to do is to network and get your business plan referred. In terms of the industries we look for, we try to keep the next thing we are looking for in mind so we can recognize an opportunity when we see it. So we quietly were early investors in business-to-business e-commerce when everyone else was busy investing in business-to-consumer. We tried not to get swayed into the business-to-consumer space because most of our partners really don't have that expertise. We are all ex-operators out of business-to-business like companies. The same is true in the communications equipment space. Once you get a critical mass of certain types of companies in your portfolio you know where the next hole is. This is very helpful because you can filter it through your portfolio companies pretty quickly and see what they think.

What do you look for in a defensible business model? Does it have to be a proprietary technology?

We would prefer that, it is kind of the NEA model, but it is not the case with venture capital firms in general. We always look at the management team and the market opportunity. Technology is great, but if the market opportunity and management team aren't there, it makes it tough. The business-to-consumer e-commerce world is much more focused on marketing and branding and getting out there first. We look much more to models that are leveraging technologies in unique ways that will really differentiate them in the long run. Whenever we invest we always ask the question: Can this be a large, sustaining, stand-alone business? And if we can't answer this question as yes, then we don't invest. If you look at our portfolio, we have 35 companies with market capitalizations over $1 billion that have created 400,000 jobs and produce $40 billion in annual revenues. These are the numbers that we are proud of, we don't look to build companies and flip them.

What are some of the sectors that you are looking to get into right now?

We are really focused right now on business-to-business e-commerce, like everyone else. But I think we were one of the early ones to invest in this space and we already have 28 companies in our portfolio doing this. We have always focused on companies that are using the Internet to build, create, or solve a problem that could never have been done without the Internet. Just taking a business model and shaving some costs and putting it online is not attractive to us. We want opportunities that are significantly revolutionizing a particular market or segment. For example, we have a company called EqualFooting.com that is focused on helping small blue-collar businesses capitalize on the powers that larger businesses have, such as purchasing departments and the ability to submit RFQ's online. These are the types of opportunities we are looking for that really change the way a market works.

What types of companies do you feel are good candidates to get such a large infusion of cash at such an early stage?

I think whenever you have an e-commerce company focused on a big market opportunity, there are going to be 20 other people thinking about the same thing. Therefore the race is on and the key for us is to back the right team and give them the money to run like crazy. It is a little different in the business-to-business marketplace versus the business-to-consumer marketplace because it is not just buying advertising, it's partnerships, and you have got to earn the trust of your constituents. In business-to-business, the other major thing to build is a customer support platform. Consumers can forgive eBay for being down for three days, but in the business world if that happens you lose those customers forever. So business-to-business companies need to spend more on traditional things like customer support and triple-redundant systems that will never go down. Another place where we invest a lot of money is in communications. To build a significant proprietary technology is complicated stuff and you have to hire 100 engineers as fast as you can who ultimately have to build it as fast as they can. Speed is really the advantage these startups have over the Lucents and Nortels of the world, because they can move on the opportunity much more quickly when they have the capital behind them.

How important are partnerships in a company's early stages?

They are extremely important. For example, EqualFooting.com has two sets of partnerships. One for marketing, to get to small businesses because they are so fragmented, and another with the brick and mortar stores for fulfillment and distribution. There is going to be much more of a marrying of the back-end brick and mortar stores with the front-end business-to-business stores because you can't build the distribution system without them. The key to partnerships is locking them up quickly and integrating with them. There are a million types of partnerships out there but you need to make ones that have a real economic impact.

How quickly do you like to see your companies become profitable?

In the old days, it used to have to be sooner because the public markets would not be very accepting of a company with a negative bottom line. But nowadays it is not that crucial because growing the top line is so much more important, at least in the Internet world. As long as you have a model that is proven that can make money, and the only reason you are not making money is because you are spending to increase the top line, you are okay. It is all about getting market share. I think everyone is forgoing profits right now because it is such a land-grab, but you have to have a model that can eventually be very profitable. There will be a shakeout at some point and the companies that get hurt the most will be the ones that do not have sustainable business models. Right now most people do not understand which models are going to win so they are betting on them all. We really look for companies with high margins, because the higher the margins, the more room you have for error. We don't have a mandate that our companies be profitable specifically in the third or fifth year, but certainly within five years their business should be at least cash-flow positive. We prefer companies that can get to cash-flow break even a year or two after they start selling. But a company may make a conscience decision not to do this, because of market factors such as a land-grab, and forgo the profit for a longer period of time.

What do you think are some of the sectors that are going to be the most promising?

Right now optical networking is very hot. I invested in a company called Quantum Bridge Communications about a year and a half ago that is now one of the hottest companies in their space. Anything broadband is really a fantastic sector to be in. Everyone talks about the market crashing but if you think back to the Industrial Revolution or any other revolution, they all lasted for quite some time. Everything with the Internet really just started in 1995. We especially like wireless, broadband, and anything that continues to push the Internet to more people and makes it more useable and faster. These are going to be what create opportunities for some time to come.

JONATHAN GOLDSTEIN
TA Associates

Jonathan Goldstein focuses on Internet and healthcare-related investment opportunities for TA Associates. Prior to joining TA Associates in 1986, Jonathan worked in the Protein Chemistry and Cell Biology Departments of Biogen, Inc. He has been published on the subject of the scale-up of recombinant animal cells, and holds a U.S. patent. He serves on the Board of numerous leading Internet and healthcare related companies.

A small sample of companies TA has invested in include Network Associates, Andover.Net, BSQUARE Corporation, Direct Hit Technologies, JDA Software, Hummingbird, SNSYS, Axent, Colorado Memory, Diamond Multimedia, Network Appliance, Ultatech Stepper, Copley Pharmaceutical, Concentra Managed Care, Gulf South Medical Supply, Boron LePore, CompDent, Private Business, AIM, Mutual Risk Management, Keystone, Affiliated Managers Group, TSR Wireless, SBA Communications, Continental Cablevision, Galaxy Telecom, Bachtel Cellular, PowerBar, Jenny Craig, Natrol, Car Toys, United Pet Group, Conley Canitano, Diversified Collection Services, Federal Express, Smith Alarm, and TechForce.

Tell me a little about your background.

I was originally a genetic engineer, doing my Masters thesis at a company called Biogen, which interestingly enough was a company that TA started back in 1978, when I decided to apply to business school. At the time, the scientists at Biogen were not happy with the business people, and the business people were not happy with the scientists. The scientists were upset that the business people were creating milestones that would get Biogen the next milestone payment, but the milestones had little to do with moving the overall project along. The business people were upset with the scientists because the scientists said that the next milestone would take six months, and three years later, it still hadn't happened. I figured that I could be someone who could bridge the two groups. I applied to business school, and although they admitted me, they wanted me to get more working experience first. I asked some of my advisors at MIT what they suggested, and I was fortunate that they put me in touch with some venture capitalists. Back then, "venture capital" was a much less familiar term, and I happened to get lucky by ending up at TA. After business school, I returned to TA and have been here ever since.

Tell me about the investment philosophy of TA.

TA was founded in 1968 and is one of the oldest venture capital firms. We are now calling ourselves "growth capital" instead of "venture capital." In the early days, venture capital had a risk connotation to it, which was appropriate for what we were doing at the time, which was early-stage investing. Then we started focusing on later-stage, profitable company investments in the late 1980's when we found that our investments in profitable companies provided better returns than our investments in early-stage companies. In business school, they teach you that if risk is priced appropriately, the more risk you take, the more you should be compensated over a whole portfolio of investments. Although any given investment may either have great returns or go to zero, over an entire portfolio, you should be compensated more for taking on greater risk. However, during that period, we found that risk was not being priced appropriately, and that we were able to produce top-tier returns for the venture capital industry while taking on much less risk than the rest of our industry. We were investing in companies that were already profitable and a lot less risky than startups. We recognized that the venture capital industry in the late 1980's and early 1990's was just pricing risk incorrectly. We figured, why would you take more risk and get lower returns? This allowed us to invest a lot more money, because when you invest in later-stage companies, you are not the VP of business development to each company, but rather a helpful director, which is theoretically something we can do better across many companies while investing more money. I like to think of it as a 25-fold different return on effort because you are managing five times as much money per investment and you spend one-fifth the amount of time on the individual investments. In addition, the time we spend on each company is targeted where we can be helpful. We are not trying to take on the responsibilities of officers of these companies—rather, we are trying to help them with strategic direction.

eBrandedBooks.com
Get Published!

So, for a while we invested almost exclusively in later-stage companies, and as one of my colleagues likes to say, "that was one of the better strategies in the our industry until Al Gore invented the Internet." And then what happened, of course, was that companies that were earlier-stage were able to generate incredibly attractive returns. So we tried to think very carefully about how we could participate in segments of this new economy because those companies, of course, were not profitable yet. The first Internet investments we made were actually in profitable companies like Datek—that was an example of our older strategy applied to this newer area. The valuation methodology, however, was very much from the new economy, and was not the simple single-digit multiple of EBITDA that typically is done. We figured out we had to find a way to participate at early-stage investing, not just with companies that are profitable. For us, profitability is really a proxy for several other things that we have historically found attractive about businesses. For example, you can look at the revenues already and recognize whether they are recurring or non-recurring revenues. You can look at gross margin and see what the trends are there as well. There are a variety of other factors, and we have learned in profitable company investing to separate the companies we like from those we don't. So in June of 1999, we decided to add to our portfolio some revenue-stage companies that were not yet profitable. It made sense because many of these companies were in a land-grab and were losing money, but they had already demonstrated that their businesses could be profitable. In this way we applied our profitable company model to early-stage investing.

What are some examples of companies you have since invested in?

We invested in a company called Direct Hit, where one of the founders is a friend I have known for 18 years. Even before we invested, I had been advising him on strategic matters regarding his company just because he was a good friend. I had a little bit of an epiphany when another friend who actually ended up being a co-investor in Direct Hit sold his company, Four11, to Yahoo in late 1997. He called me one night and asked for my advice on an offer from Lycos for $40 million—back when $40 million meant something—versus what he was anticipating to be a $50 million offer from Yahoo the following day. My advice to him was to get an advisor because the one to two percent that it would cost would pay for itself many times over because of what he'd learn in terms of hedging strategies and ultimately get in extra dollars on the price. Ultimately, they sold the company to Yahoo for $95 million in Yahoo stock. Of course, they sold it for a much higher price than the first offer, because the Yahoo stock at the time was perceived to be considerably overvalued. Needless to say, that was about fifteen-fold ago. The ironic part is that at the time, TA could not have even invested in his company because they were not profitable. He then mentioned that we should take a look at a company called Finisar, which we subsequently made an investment in and has been a great investment for us. The point was that we started seeing firsthand how tremendous value was being created in early-stage companies and how we could take advantage of it. Direct Hit was a revenue-stage company that we liked because they had a real network effect—what you call a "virtuous business cycle." Direct Hit's approach to search was to use all of the efforts of previous searchers in order to bubble-up the results that previous searchers found more valuable, and then bubble-down the ones they found less valuable. Direct Hit's results therefore become more and more relevant for users with each search that is done. We invested in that company in July, 1999, filed for a public offering in December, and sold the company to Ask Jeeves in February, 2000. I thought that was Internet time, which was about six months from start to finish. That investment was made in 11 days, and for us, we had to show an ability to turn on a dime—and we did.

Then in September, we invested in a company called Andover.net. Andover is a leading aggregator of Linux destination sites such as Slashdot.org, which is a must-read for anyone in the technical space. We made the investment in Andover over a period of three weeks. The management team at Andover indicated to us they were very close to filing to go public, but they wanted to bring in some extra cash to firm up their balance sheet. When they filed their public offering, they wanted to have an audit that would validate that Andover had all the cash necessary to meet the going concern test. Before our investment, they had made a couple of acquisitions that called for contingent payments that, at the time, they did not have the cash on hand to meet on schedule. Even though the public offering would solve this problem, the audit would take place before that cash was raised. Andover's existing investors were kind enough to let us make the investment, and the company filed for an initial public offering the next day. It was an unusual public offering because Andover serves the Linux community, which is an open source, and Red Hat had a bit of controversy previously in issuing shares. Andover decided to use WR Hambrecht, which was a new firm using a new methodology for issuing shares on the IPO called the "open IPO," which was fundamentally a Dutch auction. It did get shares to anybody who bid high enough, however, it turned out that the process was not entirely smooth: It was WR Hambrecht's first offering with a very hot security. We invested on September 15th, they filed on September 16th, they went public on December 6th. We did an acquisition between the filing and their offering, and another acquisition subsequent to the public offering in January, and then announced a merger in early February with VA Linux. That was over a four-month period. If you contrast that with how we operated only a couple of years ago, a four-month period would have been the amount of time we needed just to make the initial investment.

How is the size of the investments you make changing?

The real issue in a firm like ours, and others—although they may think about it differently—is allocation of people. We've got 12 managing directors and a few principals and vice presidents, but this is a relatively small number of people who are experienced enough to sit on a portfolio company's board of directors. Even though we are one of the bigger firms, there is only so much money that an individual firm can manage and still be a good director. And our philosophy is that—more than anything else—we strive to be good directors. That's what we want to be, that's what we hope people say about us. We hope people know that they can always count on us to do the key background work. Other firms have different strategies where they make investments but do not put people on the boards of the companies in which they invest; we, however, are on the boards of 98 percent of our investments. So the real issue is not the size of the investment—although people do pay attention to that. The real issue is the opportunity for capital gain. In other words, if you can invest $50 million and make three times your money in a short period of time, that is a great investment. That is a $100 million gain, and if you can do that over a two- to three-year period of time, that is definitely worth your time. If you can invest $10 million and make 10 times your money over the same amount of time, that's also a $100 million gain, and it's worth allocating a person to specifically manage the investment. I would argue it is the potential size of the gain that justifies the allocation of our resources, not the size of the investment. We have recognized that smaller investments have to have a higher potential return multiple than do larger investments in order to justify personnel…but that's because our limiting resource is people.

Tell me how you approach valuations and how they have changed over the last number of years.

It's always been an art more than a science, although it was probably as scientific as it ever got in the early 1990s. At that point, you could look at a company that was growing at 20 percent, look at the EBITDA, multiply it by five, six, seven, or eight, and then subtract the debt—that was what the equity was worth. Now, you can read the public company analyst reports and find five different ways to try to justify the values of some of these Internet companies. One of the things that drives us in our valuation analysis today is determining fundamentally if a company is a property that others will want to own and want to pay a high valuation for. If this is the case, then we can pay a higher valuation ourselves. I think the history of our business, despite the fact that we invest in growing companies and get some return by paying down debt, is you buy in at one multiple and you hope to sell at another multiple and if the company is growing in between you are going to get good returns and these two multiples are in your favor. There have been times when they have been inverted, which is not a good time to invest a lot of money. And because there is a time delay, you never know.

In the case of Direct Hit, we paid an enormously high price by any historical measures; we were in at about a $125 million post-money valuation. At the time, this was a company with a couple of million dollars' worth of revenue. But when we made the investment, Ask Jeeves was trading at about $900 million in market valuation and we though Direct Hit was well positioned compared to Ask Jeeves in the consumer search business. Inktomi, which was providing OEM search services to other sites to run their searches—which Direct Hit was also doing—was valued at the time at about $4 billion. So we though $125 million was off the scale on any historical basis for TA, but we were comfortable because Inktomi and Ask Jeeves were comparable public investments we could use both for an IPO and if we ended up being acquired. Ask Jeeves eventually ended up acquiring us. So you kind of do it on relative valuations.

What about when you don't have a comparable public investment to get at an approximate valuation?

When you don't have something comparable, then you don't have something entrepreneurs can hang their hat on. If you could look back at the business plans of some of these really successful companies and see what their true goals and aspirations were, you would see that they never projected their companies would be worth as much as they are now. And they certainly never predicted that they would be worth so much so quickly.

How do these valuations affect entrepreneurs who are starting companies?

It has affected the pre-money valuation of companies. People with "just an idea" used to get around $3 million dollars pre-money valuation. When an investor put in $1 million, he or she would own a quarter of the company on a post-money valuation. People with an idea now can have a pre-money valuation of $10 million dollars; people with an idea, an operating history, some employees and revenues, and a classic Series A can get a valuation in the 'teens. A Series B, or second round, could be in the $20 to $30 million range, and a Series C could be in the $60 million range. If there is a Series D, it could reach the low hundreds of million dollars. If you're public, it's in the hundreds, and then it trades up to the billions. I think we've seen huge inflation in companies where there is something comparable that's already gone public because they are just trying to move the private pricing up to the public level. We've always tried to argue that our role is one of the value-added investor who does the heavy lifting and provides the essential references. One of the things we try to make entrepreneurs realize is that if they are selling only a small portion of the company, the valuation we pay for that small part is insignificant relative to the value that we can add for the larger portion of the company.

What have the Internet and technology done to the world of venture capital?

It's like a tale of two cities. The perfect example is something that happened on the West Coast: Two very well respected firms split off into separate Internet and healthcare components because they couldn't agree on where the firm should spend their time and dollars. What we have seen in the industry with regard to the Internet and technological revolution is tension within the individual firms. We have been lucky, perhaps, in our firm that people have kept their wits about them. Just because you made a couple of investments in Internet companies that went very well, we can all still see the benefit of being a part of a larger family. I think there are also things that we have learned across many lines of business that help us in investing in the Internet space. It is a challenge because we have so many people making these decisions. In fact, our whole firm is charged with finding deals, and nobody likes to have to make an investment in only three weeks. But the fact is—when you *can* make an investment in three weeks—that is pretty appealing as well, because investments are hard to make. Over the years at TA, we have had different people have the hot hand in all different types of industries such as software, financial services,

eBrandedBooks.com
Get Published!

Internet, healthcare services, and others. And basically all of us feel we are better off to be part of a diversified firm.

Where do you see some of the best opportunities in the Internet and technology space?

Business-to-business versus business-to-consumer is overblown. I see it as the headline without the story. A lot of people at the moment hate business-to-consumer. But just because there are some reasons to hate companies in the business-to-consumer space does not mean you should hate all those types of companies. The real issue with business-to-consumer and business-to-business is a comparison between cost of customer acquisition and the lifetime value of that customer. The classic business-to-consumer company is a retailer, and has to get on television because it is one of the best mediums by which to reach lots of customers. But television advertising is very expensive per customer acquired, and the lifetime value of the customer in terms of the contribution margin generated is still not *that* much, because the business is still a retailer. They may buy a product now but not come back to your site for ten years. For example, Furniture.com is getting a lot of excitement, but how often do people buy sofas and what is the lifetime value of their customer? Drugstore.com may be a better model, because people need to buy prescriptions and drugstore items every month or so. Their lifetime value as a customer is better because they may be spending more on a recurring basis. The thing I am still not that keen on, although the market thinks otherwise, is that I don't use *more* shaving cream just because I am a Drugstore.com customer. It is incredibly convenient and I have moved my market share to them, but I do not use more of it. Now let me contrast that to Datek. I used to trade maybe ten times a year. Now I have Datek on my screen at all times with their streamer flashing at me to alert me to situations where I might want to make more trades. And so the number of trades I make in a year has now gone up significantly. So when you look at business-to-consumer, the real issue is looking at the cost to acquire customers and the lifetime value of the contribution margin of that customer. Many business-to-consumer concepts fail there, when it costs too much to get a customer and the real value of the customer is not there, and ultimately they will run out of capital. Contrast it with business-to-business: You might have a much more narrow group of customers, and therefore you know that you have to go after these 500 in a very targeted way, so it doesn't cost as much to actually acquire the customers. Then the lifetime value of a customer from a contribution margin standpoint is also much higher, because in the business-to-business space, people are typically re-ordering monthly. I think you have a lot of people who talk about business-to-business and business-to-consumer, but do not take it to that next level of analysis. There will be people on the business-to-consumer side that take it to that next level that are incredibly successful. However, if you put 1,000 business-to-business companies next to 1,000 business-to-consumer companies, will they do better on average? In my opinion, yes.

What do you see as some of the key indicators to watch that will drive the future opportunities of the Internet?

I have DSL at home and a T1 at work. Everything is becoming so inexpensive and accessible that the demand just increases. For $50 a month, I have broadband at home. But, now that I have it, I am doing all sorts of things that I never did in the past. I set up a video conference call with my Dad for free. I have a $100 camera and a $7 microphone that sit on my computer, so all I need to do is download a little piece of software and we are talking to each other on a videoconference for free. And I can conference in a number of other people as well. You can easily see the demand for this whereby once a week we get everyone on the computer, from any location, for free. The bottom line is that the cheap access just creates more demand—like MP3 files, for example. It is kind of like when AOL first offered unlimited Internet access instead of paying by the minute; I think broadband is at this stage right now. Clearly, the companies that are in broadband feel that even though all the pundits question what will happen if the cost goes to $0, it can't go to $0 or these companies would not be doing so well. It is going to be low enough that demand keeps going up. And those companies that help with infrastructure for broadband are currently all valued through the roof. I happen to think that your computer is not so much a computational device as it is going to be a communications device in the long term.

What are some of the challenges that Internet and technology companies are facing right now?

I think everyone's challenge is hiring and retaining personnel. I think hiring good people and retaining them and motivating them is something that everyone is dealing with. Every hot company may have its moment of fame, but at some point, when it's public, people will no longer have the opportunity to get in before they IPO and get the pick-up. There is an incredibly successful company in our area called Sycamore Networks, and it is a phenomenal success story. The company went public and is now suddenly valued at $30 billion dollars. That is tremendous. But I can't help but wonder, "How do you attract employees when the opportunity for appreciation may have largely occurred already?" It is such a great name, story, and run by such a great person that maybe they are still able to hire, but I am sure it is still a challenge. Perhaps the talent will seek out the next startup and try to get in before the price runs up. I also see the hiring crunch affecting conventional business that are losing employees rapidly to the Internet space. And, in the short term, they are having a very difficult time competing. Headhunters used to be doing anything to capture the attention of venture capitalists because we were often a source of business for them. They are at a point where they don't return calls for days because they are too busy. You even see venture firms hiring headhunters internally. We are now getting very involved in the recruiting space for our companies. For example, with Direct Hit, I interviewed—or more realistically, marketed to—all of the VP-level people who came in after our investment. In the case of Andover, things happened so quickly that we filed our S-1 before we even had a CFO. The other thing that helps is that when you bring on a big time venture capital firm it indicates to employees and potential hires that the company is really going somewhere. That sponsorship makes it easier to hire.

What are some of the key indicators that the Internet economy is changing, for better or worse?

We are in the middle of this frenzy—we are seeing gas prices go through the roof, and we are going to see inflation going up, which should ultimately effect the high-priced securities. You have to be able to take advantage of a multiple that is given to you because you *can*. I have been fortunate to be the beneficiary of some companies that are public at high multiples; you can acquire private companies by issuing relatively little common stock. I was with a CEO of a biotech company that just raised a billion dollars. None of the money managers can understand the value of the security, but he told me he was going to go out and raise a billion dollars because he could, and then go out and justify the market valuation he was given with that capital. I think this is a good strategy. If you are blessed with currency, you should go use it—because someday you may not have that currency to use. I think there are a lot of CEO's who are more conservative even though they have that currency, and I am not sure that that is the best way to create value for the shareholders in the long run, ironically.

What effect are options having on retaining employees? Does it help to stretch out vesting periods?

Stretching out vesting helps in holding onto people who you have hired before public offerings. There is a problem—and a problem you'd love to have, but a problem nonetheless—when a stock runs up out of control. Unfortunately, people don't really understand the underlying value of stock options. I am stunned and in effect recommend to all of my companies that they can't fight the fact that all that people think about is the number of options they have, not the percentage ownership of the overall company and what the company as a whole is worth. People don't want to hear about the value, just the number they own. They want 10,000 options. They don't care about the percentage. It is an indictment of the mathematics programs in our schools, but I guess the lottery is already evidence of that. However, I am tired of trying to explain it. So now we just split the shares 10-to-1 and give somebody 10,000 shares. I have told myself for years that I don't want to hire anybody who doesn't recognize the difference, but the economy is so hot that we have run out of those people. It has actually become a marketing issue for these companies in order to have more shares to issue.

Do you have cases where entrepreneurs come in looking for X million, and you end up suggesting to them that they need double that X million?

About once a day. Let's say that someone is thinking about selling 30 percent of their company for $10 million, which would mean a pre-money value of $20 million and a post of $30 million. Most think that if they sold $20 million, they would be selling 50 percent of their company, but I am not sure that math applies in this space. I am not sure that people are as rigorous when they raise the amount because they still need to have a motivated team, and the price per share will actually go up the more you raise. People realize you must have enough equity left over to have a motivated team.

Is it better to raise more or less in any given funding round?

It is always our interest for a company to raise more money. We are going to do all the heavy lifting anyway, and I would rather do it for a $20 million investment than a $10 million investment. The issue for the company is one of valuation. Someone does not want to be diluted because of the extra portion of the company that is issued at that point in time. So if you raised all the capital the company would ever need, you would end up owning a much smaller percentage than if you had waited to do another round later on. But there's an unusual phenomenon in the Internet space that does not exist in traditional space, and that is the value attributed to market share leadership. Let's take the valuation methodology as price-to-revenues or -to-customer accounts or whatever methodology you want to use to compare it to other companies. The company may be twice as big but six times the market valuation because the multiple is three times bigger. The multiple is three times bigger because there are unusual aspects to the Internet valuations where the "firstest with the mostest" applies. Look at Slashdot, for example, where the users are generating the content—those users aren't going anywhere else because it just keeps getting better for them. If there was someone else relative to Slashdot that had a tenth of the users they are going to have a 1/30th of the market value. So that argues to a company that you don't do a two million first round, you do a ten million round because it is a big enough space to invest the capital and be perceived as a market leader. The reason is that getting ahead and being perceived as being ahead feeds on itself. And yes, it could be that, mathematically, the most efficient thing in terms of the percentage of the company you hold onto is to raise the amount of money instantaneously as you need it, in ever-smaller slices as you go on. But if you are trying to maximize the value of the portion of the company you hold onto, you really want to be the "firstest with the mostest" and raise a lot of money up front. In addition, you are more likely to get corporate partnerships that way, more likely to have to not worry about raising money again in six months, and you will have the effect of being perceived as ahead of all your competitors. You will find that that is a better strategy for maximizing the value of what you own even if you only end up owning a fraction of what you would have the other way.

How much of a funding strategy should an entrepreneur have from the start?

It varies so much from business-to-business. Some funding strategies try to create brand through advertising. To me, that is a risky funding strategy: If your advertising does not work, you are out the money and have nothing to show for it. Then there are funding strategies where you end up with an underlying asset, which could potentially be useful to someone someday. Therefore, your company may not ultimately survive, but you can cover some of your investment value because you have created an asset that someone will care about. This can result in us having a decent investment even if the company may not have been a success. We have had some investments that have not been successful on an operating or competitive capacity that were sold more or less at cost and then the other company triples in value and our investment turns out to be pretty good.

How can management keep their entire team motivated as they grow so quickly?

This is probably the most important thing we try to help them with. The reason it is important is because we own shares in the company. Fundamentally, what motivates us is to see the value of all the shares as high as possible. We are not the ones with our hands on the steering wheel and foot on the gas pedal—that is the job of the management team. To be a good director, you need to help set the company's strategy, helping with the IPO process, helping with positioning, and becoming familiar with legal and options issues. Part of it is making people feel that they are part of something bigger and giving people credit where they deserve it. I think it is always a mistake, as someone in the venture capital industry, to take credit for anything. One of my most important learning experiences was with a CEO I backed at Gulf South Medical Supply. He always was the last to take credit for something and the first to give credit to someone else. This is a great way to motivate people. You obviously have the financial methods to motivate people but you have to make them feel like valued contributors, because they are valued contributors. And frankly, you have got to go the other way as well. If they are not valued contributors you have to replace them. These are companies that can afford to "wait and see" with people who are not getting it done.

How is a company well managed?

Attracting key employees, motivating key employees, coming up with smart financing strategies, taking advantage of what is given to you, being able to be nimble and adjust strategies when necessary, handle and deal with competitive threats, and being able to deal with moral and ethical issues just to name a few. It is no different than other non-Internet businesses, but, in general, you have individuals who are young and inexperienced. That does not mean that they cannot be great executives, it just takes some time.

Tell me about one or two companies you admire.

I think eBay is a great company. I think they are a classic example of a virtuous cycle and they just become stronger. You may be able to compete with eBay in a very deep niche, but no one will be able to compete with them on a broad basis. I think Yahoo has done a tremendous job in leveraging its community into other things. I think Amazon has done a fantastic job by realizing it is tough to make a lot of money on the gross margin of just selling books or some of the other products they have gotten into. But Amazon really makes a lot of money in the fact that it is a mall. A partner will pay Amazon $80 million just to get a button on their site. I think they have done a good job at that, and have also modified their strategy well over time.

VIRGINIA BONKER
Blue Rock Capital

Before co-founding Blue Rock Capital, Virginia served as Vice President of the Sprout Group, the Venture Capital affiliate of Donaldson, Lufkin & Jenrette. Previously, she was with DLJ's Investment Banking Group and at Hewlett Packard.

Blue Rock Capital has invested in companies such as Midas Vision, NexTone Communications, Tellium, NxtWave Communications, beMANY!, Channel Wave, Fact City, Gain Capital, Grocery Works, justballs, museumshop.com, Entigo, trainingnet.com, Integrated Chipware, Lockstar, NetBalance, Response Networks, Edison Schools, and Momentum Partners.

How has the venture capital world changed in the last few years with all this new attention being paid to it?

The Internet has changed everything, especially the venture capital world. With the influx of capital, there's now a lot of money chasing a lot more deals. Over the last dozen or so years that I have been doing this, it has really changed from being an old boys club—where there were only a handful of venture firms and many fewer companies being started—to now, where there is a lot more activity on both sides of the equation. It is a much more frenetic market than it ever has been in the past.

How much harder is it finding deals now than it was in the past?

There are many dynamics working with that question. One is that there is certainly a lot more competition in the sense that there is a lot more venture capital. There are also a lot more businesses being started, so there is a lot more opportunity to put money to work as well. Personally, I've had an easier time putting money to work in good companies now versus five years ago, because my network of relationships at top venture firms has grown over that time. This is just a case in point that business is personal. For a venture capitalist or an entrepreneur, your network is everything.

What is the most exciting part of being a venture capitalist?

Working with the entrepreneurs, for sure. You have people who are very smart and energetic, and have a vision. My parents are entrepreneurs, so I grew up in an environment where every day was a new challenge and struggle, and also a joy. To be able to be involved with 15 or 20 companies that are going through high growth is exhilarating. It is also intellectually very stimulating because the companies are working in different industries. Whether they are in software, telecom, or the Internet, they have different business models and marketplaces. I can't think of anything that's more interesting to do than help companies as they're growing and serve their needs. No wonder everyone wants to be a venture capitalist. Then again, there are downsides to it as well. Not all of these rocket ships will make it to the moon.

It seems like venture capitalists that are consistently involved in so many deals must lead a very frenetic life. What is a typical week like for you?

My week definitely has a rhythm to it. Generally, I'm traveling on Tuesdays, Wednesdays, and Thursdays and I try to be in the office on Mondays and Fridays. That can change but, in general, I am traveling to New York, Boston, or DC for board meetings. For each of these days, the board meeting usually lasts two to four hours and I try to bundle in two or three additional meetings. The key objective is to talk to good people, even if I may not know where they might fit in my life at any given time, because the best deals come as referrals from either my network of entrepreneurs or venture firms. I do try to be in the office at least one or two days a week just because of the volume of stuff that needs to be processed to stay on top of the requests from our portfolio companies. I spend a lot of time helping our companies with recruiting, financings, strategy, and governance issues like stock options.

Tell me about the investment philosophy of your firm and how it differs from other types of venture capital firms.

Blue Rock is a $51 million fund for seed and early-stage IT focused companies. What makes us different is that we are very well connected to the larger top-tier funds. We are first-round investors and we work closely with our companies because that's what we love doing. The bigger funds can't do that because there are just too many companies they have invested in. We also have the ability within the first or second round to bring on the deep pockets that companies need to move in web time. So I think that we are in a special place in the market because so many venture firms have raised very large funds. For a company that needs $1 million to $2 million to get to the next level, or even $3 million to $5 million, a lot of the top-tier firms can't look at something that small. However, because we have such great relationships with them, they often say "okay, we'll put in a million or two with you and know you'll work with the company closely so that we'll have the chance to put in $10 or $15 million in the next round."

So when other VCs co-invest with you they are comfortable because you have already done the due diligence and are going to be working closely with the company?

We share all our due diligence with potential co-investors. We each make our separate decision that this looks good and we are going to invest. It is also a great way for them to remain active in seed and early-stage funding even if they're managing a billion dollar fund.

Tell me about a recent investment in an Internet company you have made.

We just made an investment in a company called beMANY! with Softbank and Bertelsmann. It is a business-to-business and business-to-consumer e-commerce play in buyer aggregation for services run by one of the top people from Vertical Net. As most venture firms will tell you, it is the people that are the most important in early stage investing. In this case we felt very strongly about the capabilities, vision, and drive of the CEO.

What are some of the specific characteristics you're looking for in a management team when you're looking to make an early-stage investment?

The first thing is integrity, because at the end of the day, you have to trust each other. There will always be a lot of ambiguity and judgment calls, so you have to think that the person has high integrity and good judgment. The second thing is that they are very smart and very driven to build something of significant value. Lastly, I think that you have to feel as if they're able to build a team around them and execute. One person, no matter how driven or smart, will not be able to make anything very exciting happen if they can't make the other people feel empowered.

How far along does an entrepreneur have to be in his or her idea for you to consider an investment?

Nothing is too early for us. We will invest in a team and a dream, or even one person and a vision. For example, beMANY! did not have a web site up when we made the investment and there was no tangible product. Their management team, however, had a very clear vision and had demonstrated in the past their ability to execute and succeed. We'd love for a company to have customers or even beta users of the product but it is not necessary for us to make an investment.

There is always a lot of talk about valuations and it gets increasingly difficult when you're looking at early-stage companies. Are there any benchmarks you use in determining valuations of such early-stage companies?

You probably don't want me to tell you about the Ouija board or the coin toss. Seriously, I do think that valuation is one of those areas that entrepreneurs think is a pretty haphazard, mysterious process. I think it's really a case where the market drives valuation and if the deal is hot, the valuation is going to move up. If the deal is languishing, it's like your house being on the market too long, and it's going to be pressured downward. I also think that there is a demonstrable difference in valuation depending on what part of the country you're in. Being in Silicon Valley tends to have higher valuations in general than in the eastern part of the US—especially outside of Boston, which tends to have higher valuations than other parts of the eastern US basically because of supply and demand. A lot has happened in the past year regarding valuation because the amount of capital required for companies to compete has increased. And although its not necessarily intuitive, if a company is raising $5 million versus $1 million, the valuation tends to go up just because venture folks are not looking to own 80 percent of a company. For Blue Rock, we try to base a company valuation on some estimate of the value that has been created to date and the market potential. We take many factors into account, including the amount of cash and sweat equity that the team has invested, where the product is in its development, customers sold, partnerships signed, etc. As far as market potential is considered, if a company is addressing a large market where it has a chance of becoming the market leader, the valuation is higher than a niche play. In general, we have tried not to get caught up in the current euphoria because valuations have been pushed to ridiculous levels in some cases.

Let's say you take in angel financing in the first round, you often hear that in later rounds angels can be upset because they did not get in at the best valuation. How true is this?

Actually I believe that angels often times overpay because they're less price sensitive than institutional investors.

What sort of things should an entrepreneur trying to understand how to value their own company look at when they go out for financing? And is it something they should go to a venture capitalist and say, "this is the valuation I want for my company," or is it something they should leave more open for discussion, since it will obviously get discussed?

I think it has changed a bit because of the incredible level of activity in the marketplace. On the one hand, I used to like it when an entrepreneur said, "I'm really flexible, and the market will dictate." These days, however, one of my secrets is that venture folks generally want an entrepreneur to voice their expectations. I think the reason for this is that we're all too busy to do any work on a deal if the entrepreneur has completely outlandish expectations. So, perhaps the best answer an entrepreneur could give would be, "we've looked at comparable companies being financed at a similar stage as well as the potential market opportunity, and we believe that an X million dollar valuation is appropriate. However, our number one objective is to get the company financed with the right partners and on a timely basis." That shows that they've put thought into it and put a stake in the ground but they are not fixated on the number.

There is so much talk about business-to-business opportunities in the marketplace, but what specific areas do you like for technology companies right now?

I think buyer aggregation is a very interesting area—not just services, but products as well. The web allows individuals, whether they are small- or medium-sized businesses or consumers, to take advantage of the efficiency brought to them by being part of a community. This is the essence of the web. Another hot area is business-to-business supply chain rationalization. Taking inventories of certain industries and rationalizing a very complex and inefficient supply chain—where you might have a manufacturer, distributor, reseller, jobber, wholesale supplier, and others–is a very interesting area. A lot of these supply chains have multiple markup points and very little value added at each level. Those are perfect opportunities for the web to rationalize them. Lastly, I'm really big on community and the viral nature of the web. Some of the best business models have to do with offering something which is of value to members for free, and then offering that community, which has a common interest, products and services that they would be pleased to have put in one place for them to purchase. This is very powerful because then you have viral growth with people telling their friends.

Tell me about a business model that you really like?

I really like the business model of our buyer aggregation company, beMANY! because it really highlights the viral power of the web. Buyer aggregation is based upon transparent and dynamic pricing, so that as the group of participants gets larger, the prices paid for services go down.

It sounds a lot like Mercata. How is this different?

The main difference is that beMANY! is perpetual. We are not going to try to get a thousand people to buy VCRs and then start from square one after those thousand come and make their purchase. beMANY! is perpetual because the nature of services is different. You're buying long distance, cellular, energy, or another service that you pay for every month. So it's much more powerful than products where you don't get the benefit of the continuous growth of the group. And the viral nature of it is simply that if you tell a friend, then you and a friend both benefit by getting some amount off the next month's bill.

When an entrepreneur goes out to raise a seed or first-round, how much money should they raise?

It's totally dependent on their plan. We like to see entrepreneurs take the first year and model it out monthly. In addition, we like to see different significant milestones, such as when the web site has been developed or commerce has begun. Then, you'll see where the inflexion points for creating value are, and the company will get the appropriate step up in valuation for the next round. Everyone is pretty well aware that raising money is very time consuming. It takes the senior management out of running the business, so you don't want to have to do it that often.

Is there a rule of thumb in terms of an exact time length they should raise money for, such as two years?

Two years is too long in general. The rule of thumb is generally nine months to a year, but that's a very loose rule of thumb. There are also other ways of structuring a financing, like receiving the capital in two amounts at different times. As the business grows you achieve certain milestones that take away a tremendous amount of the upfront risk.

What sort of role does your firm play in companies that you invest in?

The first thing I should say is that we're not involved in the day-to-day operations. If we were that hands-on, the entrepreneur would want to choke us. What we do try to do is serve them in whatever way they ask us. In most cases, we serve on the board and attend monthly board meetings for each of our portfolio companies. We do like to do a lot of things for each of them, if we can, between the board meetings. For example, we are involved in things like interviewing key people. And again, we're not there to veto or to bless a specific hire, we're only there to say, "have you thought about these three things," or, "maybe when you talk to some references, you might make sure you explore this because it sounded a little funny to me." Interviewing key people is a big part of what we try to help with, because getting talent is really a challenge these days. Another thing we absolutely have to help with is future financing rounds. At any given time, two or three of our companies are probably in the midst of doing the next round of financing. Another important thing is helping to identify all of the interconnections between our portfolio companies and where they could help each other. These interconnections, whether they are strategy, partnerships, or just ideas, are the key to succeeding as an Internet company. It is basically just sharing experiences and contacts from one company to another that they can all benefit from.

How do you create value as a startup Internet company?

Well, you have to think about it in the context of the business vision and model. What is proprietary and unique? There has to be some level of competitive advantage and it might not be forever sustainable, but it has to be three steps ahead of the competition. From there, the company needs to be constantly innovating in order to remain ahead. I'll give you one example. One of our e-commerce companies is MuseumShop.com and they have exclusive contracts with 35 museums to be their e-commerce partner. Now, that's very powerful. Another thing that's powerful is that they have put together an exclusive partnership with Antenna Audio, the largest provider of audio-taped tours for museums in the world. Because of this particular partnership, when they go to blue chip museums—like the Louvre and the Vatican—with Antenna who has worked with them for the last fifteen years, they will have a much easier time making the sale. These are examples of value-creating activities that one Internet startup did that created proprietary value in line with its business vision.

Because I am sure you see so many business plans, what catches your eye and really makes you want to take notice? Is it important that they submit a fifty-page business plan for example?

Definitely not a fifty-page business plan. I'm looking for an executive summary that is somewhere between three and five pages, which lays out the vision and the management team. We actually have on our web site (at bluerockcapital.com) exactly what we'd like an executive summary to cover. It makes a big difference to me if I can see that somebody has actually done his or her homework. If I get a spammed business plan, it doesn't even get responded to. Maybe that's another VC secret: most unsolicited business plans don't get read because VCs get so many of them every day. What an entrepreneur must do is know someone who knows me. There has to be one degree of separation, or I don't have time to read it. And so that means they have to network enough in the entrepreneurial community to get there. Networking is so underrated by entrepreneurs that have never been venture funded before. Those who have been venture funded before know the game, which is basically that you have to find a way to be in the network. And you can get in the network, it's just that you have to put in the effort by asking people to breakfast, lunch, and dinner and seeking out the council of people who are in the flow of high growth businesses. For example, go to one of the venture banks like Silicon Valley Bank and find a banker who will hear your story. If they're sold on it, they will call up one of their venture friends and give a good referral.

It's an interesting point you make about referrals. So many people think that if they send their plan out to enough venture capitalists, they'll get a response. What other ways are there for entrepreneurs to really network themselves in getting to know these people?

It is a case where they should figure out who the players are in their industry. If they're in a telecom area, they should be aggressively pursuing luminaries in their industry. I had one guy who came to me, and I was really impressed that he had five advisors who were big name people in his

eBrandedBooks.com
Get Published!

industry. He was just incredibly resourceful with making phone calls to people who he wanted to get to know and getting them involved. He just figured out, "whom do I need to convince and who's knowledgeable in the industry?" So when I see that the entrepreneur has already made this progress, it makes me think, "this guy must have something because these people have put their names on his advisory board."

There is obviously so much still happening in the way of new Internet and technological developments. What do you see as some of the key developments that are going to redefine the landscape of the marketplace once again?

BROADBAND! Suddenly the pipes will be infinitely big and the world will change. Broadband will really change everything. Suddenly your computer is going to be like your television, except better.

What sort of due diligence should entrepreneurs be doing regarding the venture capitalists that want to invest in them? Also, what are the things that the venture capitalist should be bringing to the table besides the money?

Before they make their decision about who to go with, entrepreneurs should do the same sort of intense due diligence on their potential partner that their partner is doing on them. They should ask to talk to half a dozen of the CEOs that the person who would be sitting on their board has worked with in the past. They should talk to those people and ask them how well they work together. Have they been there in good times as well as bad times? Because there will be both in the first six months. Are they a good listener? The most that we can do for our CEOs is to be there because it is lonely at the top. No matter how much they have built a team, ultimately they're faced with some very tough decisions. If they think that they can go to you as a board member and as a confidante, and just tell you their thoughts and ask for your advice knowing that you will be totally supportive of them whether they take your advice or not, this is a very healthy and helpful relationship.

When companies are starting out, how important are strategic partnerships for them?

That depends on their industry. Some companies need to be in stealth mode to be able to complete their product before they tell the world. However, most companies that are Internet-based need to be doing partnerships, because they are absolutely the key to success.

When you invest in companies, what is your time span in terms of looking for a return on your investment?

We believe that a three to seven year horizon is what we're in for. We're patient investors because we know that early-stage companies require time to mature. We started a fund five years ago and people were more of that mind back then. Today, people want to know why companies haven't gone public nine months into existence. We're a bit more patient than that, not to say that we're not running as hard as we can with all of our companies. It's just a case of realizing that when you're talking about true seed investing, it takes a little bit of time to get all the way up the IPO curve.

Is the ultimate goal an IPO in every one of your investments? If an entrepreneur comes to you and says they want to sell their business in three years, is that a red flag?

I would want to know why they would say that. I think that most companies in our portfolio will get sold rather than go public because of the nature of being a seed investor—just the numbers will tell you that more companies get sold than go public. But I would want to understand why somebody might say that sort of thing, because that would be something unusual to hear. Usually most people say, "I want to maximize value for all the shareholders and I will work with the board in order for all of us to decide which route we should take." So, if they just make such a blanket statement, I would wonder whether they're really collaborative to work with, and whether they really understand that when you're bringing in institutional capital, the game is to maximize shareholder value, not to take a course before it's laid out for you.

How are you encouraging, or not encouraging, your portfolio companies to expand internationally?

It depends on the company. For some companies it can be a distraction and unwise because their market opportunity may be so immense in the US, and the logistics are much more straightforward . They should not become defocused by expanding internationally in the early days. Focus is one of the absolutely critical elements of success. Then again, there are many companies in our portfolio that, at a very early age, have branched out internationally. One of our companies, called TrainingNet, is an intermediary for all things training. They do not own any of the content but facilitate the purchase of training products and services on a business-to-business basis. They become part of a corporation's intranet and allow its employees to get a course in, say, C++ in a certain place at a certain time. TrainingNet just purchased a UK-based provider because we believe that the business model is transferable to Europe and that TrainingNet will have first mover advantage by making this acquisition. So, in some cases, we aggressively pursue international expansion while in others we have been much more focused on the US opportunity.

What sort of stake are you looking to take in a company you invest in?

With this $51 million fund, our first investment is a minority stake usually between $1 to $2 million. Right now, we have 21 companies in the portfolio and that number will grow to 23 within the next month or so.

How do you personally keep track of everything developing in the industry?

It's not easy. When I'm on the road, I literally pack 20 or more magazines that I rifle through on the train or plane. And "rifle" really is the term because I don't have the luxury of reading any article, unless it immediately speaks to me from its headline. I also get selected analyst reports from Wall Street in areas where our companies are active. Our portfolio companies also send me industry material. So, to some extent, it is the companies that need to keep me up to speed.

What effect do you think venture capitalists are having on the Internet economy?

Well, if you read the press, it says that venture capitalists are the heroes. Seriously, I do think that one of the things that has made our economy so strong in the last half-dozen years is that there is a sufficient amount of risk capital available to allow for ambitious, creative, smart entrepreneurs to go for their dreams. I've lived abroad and that's not to be taken for granted. It's a wonderful advantage that America has economically, particularly regarding the rapid development of the Internet economy.

Where do you see some of the opportunities for entrepreneurs over the next couple of years as the Internet marketplace continues to change?

We are just at the beginning of seeing the power of the Internet. Both business-to-consumer and business-to-business opportunities will explode as bandwidth increases and Internet appliances become ubiquitous. Wireless

Internet will be hot. Infrastructure companies will continue to be hot. In the next couple of years, the Internet marketplace will look nothing like it does today and there will be opportunities for smart, well-connected entrepreneurs to build lasting companies.

GUY BRADLEY
CMGI @Ventures

Guy initially joined CMGI in 1994 as Director of International Marketing and Sales for BookLink Technologies. Prior to joining CMGI, Guy worked as a consultant and in Product Management and Strategic Planning at Softlab GmbH, a $100 million software development subsidiary of BMW based in Munich, Germany. Guy is now a general partner of @Ventures, a private venture capital firm affiliated with CMGI.

@Ventures has invested in companies such as Asimba.com, Mondera.com, AuctionWatch.com, MotherNature.com, BizBuyer.com, MyFamily.com, blaxxun interactive, NextMonet.com, Boatscape.com, NextOffice.com, buyersedge.com, NextPlanetOver.com, CarParts.com, Oncology.com, Craftshop.com, OneCore.com, Critical Path, PlanetOutdoors.com, Domania, Productopia, eCircles.com, Radiate, eGroups.com, Silknet Software, EXP.com, Snapfish, foodbuy.com, Speech Machines, FindLaw, SpotLife, Furniture.com, ThingWorld.com, Gamers.com, Ventro, Half.com, Vicinity, HotLinks, Virtual Ink, Intelligent/Digital, Visto Corporation, KnowledgeFirst, VStore, KOZ.com, and WebCT.

Tell me the most exciting part of being a venture capitalist.

Helping young companies and young, inexperienced entrepreneurs to grow. Deal making is fine, but what is most fun is getting in there, really understanding the business that they're in, and then helping them to be more successful at it.

Tell me a little about your background and how you ended up becoming a venture capitalist.

Well, it wasn't the shortest distance between two points, that's for sure. I worked as a programmer for several years, and then moved into project management and then product management. I also did some marketing and strategic planning and had the fortune—or misfortune, depending upon how you look at a ICASE (Integrated Computer Aided Software Engineering) tools company that was working on an incredible breadth of products. That's where I got an education in half a dozen major areas of software and applications. The company built its own multi-tasking operating system on top of DOS. It had its own windowing system with its own java-like programming language. It had a text editor, graphics editor, email package, project management tools, configuration version, but with the central system administration and configuration management tools that Java still largely lacks, and this project was back in the late 1980s. So, at various points in time as product manager, I was responsible for just about everything that didn't fall under the category of CASE tools, and as a result I became skilled in a whole bunch of different application areas. This in particular has helped me stay in good stead when interfacing with, working with, and interacting with the entrepreneurs.

So what was it that actually got you to where you are now?

I answered a four-line ad in the *Boston Globe* looking for programmers back in mid-1994 for a company called Booklink Technologies. Essentially, the ad said "Booklink Technologies, Internet startup, programmers wanted." It was a spin-off startup of a recent IPO, one of the smallest IPOs to ever have made it onto the Nasdaq, a company called CMGI. I sent in my résumé saying I didn't want to program, but if they were looking for somebody in product management or marketing, I would be interested. Shortly thereafter, David Wetherell gave me a call back—this was, of course, back before he was *the* David Wetherell. We hit it off on the phone and I came on board as director of international marketing and sales. Then three or four months later, the company was sold to AOL, and basically I opted to stay with the money rather than with the company. The proceeds from the sale were unexpectedly used to form a venture fund, @Ventures, and I was grand-fathered in as an associate. About a year and a half later I was promoted to full partner, and I currently sit on the boards of nine of our investments.

What is the essence of being a venture capitalist? What sorts of roles have VCs had in terms of helping build the Internet economy?

I think that the essence of venture capital is taking calculated risks. Although it doesn't matter how much money the companies you invest in lose for a while, ultimately they have to have a business model that works. The chances of this being the case are much higher when analysis is done by the VC up front. I don't think that there has been a great deal of conscious structuring and planning among VCs with regard to the Internet. I think back to how we went about investing in the early days of @Ventures: entrepreneurs came by, we looked at them, listened to their pitch, thought about the implications and possibilities, and then decided whether or not we wanted to invest. I think this is the same for most of my peers as well. There have obviously been some cases where individual venture capitalists or entire VC funds have gone out and tried to make specific things happen, but I think that such efforts have gone awry more often than they have succeeded. A few great companies have come out of such attempts, but there have been some real flops as well—and you never hear about the flops. During the past few years, venture capital investment in Internet companies has been less a grand plan than a genetic algorithm: we invested in a fairly random set of companies, some of them turned out to be successful, and then we used the lessons learned to direct our next round of investments. I think venture capitalists have played a critical role in the rapid formation and upswing of the Internet economy. If there hadn't been venture capital, we would probably be somewhere between a year and eighteen-months instead of five years into the Internet age. Venture capital supercharges growth and has caused things to move that much more quickly than they would have otherwise.

You hear so much about the investments that have been successful for VC firms, but you rarely hear about the unsuccessful ones. How often is it that your investments really yield these unbelievable returns that everyone is reading about?

You're lucky if two out of ten yield 20x returns or better. @Ventures has been extremely successful by VC standards but here are our rough figures for investments done between mid 1995 and mid 1998: of 21 investments done, two have returned north of 250x, three between 50 and 100x, three between 10 and 50x, five are between break-even and 5x, six are still up in the air, and in two cases we lost money. Once again, this is much better than almost all other VCs during this period.

What is your perspective on how the international landscape is developing from a technology and Internet standpoint?

What we are seeing is essentially a copycat version of what has happened in the United States. The thought is that if something has worked over in the States, it's worth doing over there. I think that's a smart way of operating because so many Internet businesses have a local component to them. Often the business is tied in closely with the language, local behavior, or a partner location. I think that, in terms of big infrastructure plays, the business has to be based in the United States since that is where almost everything happens first. Relatively few of the US dot coms that have a local component will successfully manage to spread internationally and dominate worldwide (except through acquisitions). It's a funny thing because everyone always talks about the Internet becoming one global marketplace, however, when you get down to it, most of the things that people do on the Internet really do have a lot of local specificity.

Tell me a little about the venture philosophy of CMGI.

I feel that on a day-to-day, investment-to-investment basis, there is a great deal of opportunism. There are simply so many investment opportunities that we see every day. I think we have somewhere between 3,000 and 6,000 business plans a month being sent to us. So, this vast flood of business plans is going by, and you really only have time to scan them. Every so often, one of them catches your eye for some reason. You might have read about some other company in the same space, or you might have been thinking about similar possibilities taking place in the near future. It might just be that the background of the CEO jumps out at you and makes you think that whatever this guy might do, he's going to be successful at it. When you take a look at CMGI's published investment strategy, there is a good deal of ex-post facto explanation for the ways we have invested in the past. Our website shows that we invest in four different categories, although we never set out to invest in this way. After making these investments, we made some attributions and provided some structure to them. That being said, clearly we did talk as a partnership, and there was always a great deal of thought that went into every investment. We asked ourselves what types of industries we wanted to be in, what type of business models were we looking for, what type of structure did we want in the deals, and the exit possibilities for each individual investment opportunity. To that extent, we were sensitized, prepared, and ready to invest in certain things—or at least more ready to invest in certain things than in others. However, if you take a look at the portfolios of the various partners and look at what each of them has invested in, you'll find quite different characteristics of the companies that each of us has chosen to invest in on the whole. Although we always talk about every investment, each partner makes investments in the industries and types of companies they are the most comfortable with. There has been such an incredible wave of entrepreneurial activity out there that going at things in an overly systematized way can make you lose out on an incredible number of opportunities.

How is CMGI @Ventures different than other firms?

We used to be much more different than we are now. Now, there are several other firms who work in the same way we do. What used to set us apart was that we had a clear and exclusive focus on "Internet companies." There wasn't anyone else out there that did that. Also, at the time when our venture fund was being set up, most VCs subscribed to the idea of having a broad portfolio—that is, they thought it best to make investments in a whole bunch of different areas. This was essentially to provide them with some level of downside protection if one segment or another turned out to be relatively flat for a certain period of time. The problem with that was that you had a lot of VC firms that became sort of a jack-of-all-trades—doing waste management investments today, retail tomorrow, and technology investments the next. This did not create a great deal of synergy between the various investments that they made. By concentrating on a specific area, we as partners were able to quickly build up a much greater level of expertise. This in turn made us more attractive to new investment opportunities. Perhaps most importantly, we were really able to capitalize upon the synergies between various investments and help them to work together in many instances. In fact, we now have an off-site CEO summit every six months, where the CEOs of between 70 to 80 companies in which we've invested in come together to meet. The deal making that goes on there is infectious, and we hear back, even from seasoned entrepreneurs, that they are immensely helpful events. I should make it clear, however, that what we are doing is putting executives at each of these companies in touch with each other. We don't go about it heavy-handedly, as some of the other VCs do, by insisting that portfolio companies work together. Our approach has always been that if it makes business sense, then good; if it doesn't, then don't do it, but at least hear one another out. I've found that this soft sell approach has been immensely fruitful and is really appreciated. To get back to your question, the investment focus produced an amazing number of points of contact between so many of these companies that it used to set us apart. However, now other firms such as ICG are even more narrowly focused than we are, so this point of differentiation is fading. Most firms are now seeing the wisdom of building a more focused portfolio.

When you're making an investment in a young Internet company, what type of role do you look to play?

Well, we have typically led the early-stage investments that we have made. The logic behind that is that venture capitalists are like other human beings—we have only so much bandwidth at any given time. If you're sitting on more than nine or ten boards, you can't give the companies the time and attention they need. So if you're going to be only on nine or ten boards at a time, and you want to invest as much money as possible, then you have to take a significant stake in each of those companies for them to be worth your while. We mostly did early-stage investing for the first four years of our fund, although recently we've started to do some later-stage investing. The way I look at it, the role of the venture capitalist—if it's done right—should be about 15 percent fiduciary oversight and about 85 percent broad-based consulting. Some of the consulting is specifically asked for by the company, some of it is not. The type of consulting offered really depends upon the skill sets that the individual VC brings to the table with respect to that specific deal. With my background, coming out of product management, I'm able to give advice on the technology, architecture, marketing, sales pitches, presentations, and organization structure. I will meet with new key hires to give my feedback on them as well. Each individual VC is going to have certain areas in which they excel more than others—we basically just try to help the company in any way we can by using our specific backgrounds and skills.

Take me through some of the investments you have made.

One of the most interesting was a company called PlanetAll, which allows you to stay connected with friends and business contacts regardless of how you move around. Contact information has a half-life of around two and half years these days because people switch jobs and move to new houses so frequently. What PlanetAll does is to update contact information in your contacts address books, and vice versa, whenever someone reports that it has changed. Sort of a modern replacement for change of address notes, which no one sends any more. It was originally passed along to us by another VC who looked at it and said it was "too out there" for his firm, however he knew it might be something that CMGI might be interested in so he passed it along to us. I looked at it, was intrigued, and shortly thereafter met with the CEO and CTO. There were about a dozen people working there when I first met with them, and I looked at what they were doing and immediately recognized that they really had the right way to do contact management. It makes a lot more sense for everyone to update his own information when it changes than for someone else to try to keep track of everyone else they know as they move or change jobs. We ended up investing around $5 million dollars in the company. They needed a great deal of advice, since they were first time entrepreneurs, and so I spent a lot of time with them working on both tactical and strategic issues. After about a year, they received a buyout offer from Amazon.com. The individuals who founded the company had not "made it" yet. When Amazon.com said that they would pay $100 million for it, pretty much out of the blue—and this was a couple of years ago—it was a classic offer they couldn't refuse. In fact, it turned out even better since it was a stock deal, and the share price of Amazon.com went up threefold within about six months of doing the deal.

Contrast that with Silknet, which recently went public and then was bought by Kana about 10 or 11 months later. When we invested, they were a four-person company, but the CEO had previously grown an organization from about two to 100 people and had been through an IPO before. It was an enterprise software play, and the management team came out of the enterprise software business, so they knew exactly what they wanted to do. I looked at it, thought about the whole idea and concept of customer support in the age of the Internet, and just as with PlanetAll, said, "That's the way it's going to be done." I was convinced that this was going to be a very big area. I liked the CEO and felt he was very backable and could take it all the way through to an IPO. We funded them and although I have stayed very involved with them over the years, it was much less than with PlanetAll, and has always been strategic rather than tactical.

I think that one of the myths that swirls around about venture capitalists—and many VCs actually tend to think of themselves this way—is that the VC somehow *makes* the company. That's not the way it works. The entrepreneurs make the company and it stands or falls on the basis of what the CEO, management team, and the rest of the employees do. All that the VC does is to provide a limited amount of guidance and wisdom. The company does all of the real work and this was definitely the case in both PlanetAll and Silknet.

Tell me about a more recent investment you have made.

In July, we invested in a company called Intelligent Digital down in Atlanta. When I came across them, they were close to putting together a prototype. They are developing a market exchange application aimed at Vertical Market Makers in the business-to-business infrastructure area. Back then, they were about seven or eight people; eight months later, they have a team of over a hundred. They have 65 engineers and have already released the first version of their market exchange product. Their customers are vertical market makers, such as the global food exchanges, used equipment exchanges, fuel exchanges and so on. Their basic business model is that they provide the underlying technology, which can be customized to any market. One of the nice things about doing this particular deal is that they come into contact with a huge number of early-stage business-to-business vertical market makers in which we would like to invest, so they will bring a constant source of interesting opportunities for us.

Where do you see the architecture of the Internet going from a technological standpoint?

That is a complex question because there are so many ways of answering it. Here are a few thoughts. What we're going to see is many more people having high bandwidth connections. Consequently, there will be a whole bunch of new applications. The long-awaited video-on-demand will become a reality, and there will be a lot more use of multimedia on the net, although not as much as people are thinking because the production costs for good multimedia are orders of magnitude more than plain web pages. So, most of what is on the web will continue to be the same sort of stuff that is there today. It will just be spiced up with high bandwidth and expensive content. I think that you'll see a great deal more happening with wireless and a lot of smart devices. The combination of these last two points is particularly interesting. One of the things that I think we'll be seeing increasingly more of is "intelligence." Everything that can possibly do so will come with a built-in computer chip that will enable it to communicate wirelessly with a central office or home computer. This will cause everyone's environment to become much "smarter" about things. The vision that MIT's Media Lab is promoting is someone asking, "Where are my shoes?" And the computer generated voice out of the speaker responding, "You mean the brown ones? They're in your upstairs cupboard." And that is, I think, where we are going. It won't happen immediately, but that's the direction we are heading. The "Internet appliance," which, at the moment, is a fairly narrow term, will eventually disappear since everything will be an Internet appliance one way or another. One additional corollary, eventually home networks will be just as common as office networks are today.

What are some of the specifics you look for when making an investment?

It's really a combination of things. I look for a management team, or a core of a management team, which I can either expand upon or build a foundation beneath, but at least I need to know that there is some fixed points to work with. I also look for a market opportunity that is large enough to support a public company—and not just a borderline public company, but a market which, assuming realistic penetration rates of 5 to 10 percent, can still support a billion-dollar revenue company. I look for a company which has some level of defensibility, be it proprietary technology, existing relationships with other key market players or influencers, or at least appears to have a first-mover advantage and is not too far away from being able to capitalize upon that. We also look to make first-round investments where we can get a significant chunk of the company from the beginning. These are the basic guidelines.

Take me through what you look for when you're trying to value an early-stage company.

There's a great deal less science involved than perhaps appears to be the case from the outside or from the entrepreneur's perspective. For myself, I have general ranges that I look for. If I see that this is a seed deal, it ought to be within the following range. If this is a first-round deal, it ought to be in a different range. I adjust the range into which it falls either upward or downward, depending upon the specifics of the situation. If a company's got a CEO who's been there and done it before and is eminently backable, then the company will get a higher valuation than one with an inexperienced CEO. Early-stage investments are certainly not done on the basis of ROI. Later-stage investing is a different game, and if you're investing just before the IPO, there's a whole bunch of additional analysis you can apply to get a clearer picture of what your return is likely to be. When you're doing first-round investments, it is much more a question of what the market in general is like for things at this stage, and how does this compare with an average offering?

It's interesting to hear what people say about it because it's a fascinating process. I'm sure you see entrepreneurs quite often who come in with some very inflated ideas.

Yes, and in a way that attitude harms rather than helps them. It harms them in the sense of their ultimate valuation as well, not just whether or not they get funded, because they haven't been realistic. What you need to do as an entrepreneur is to come in quoting an ideal valuation that is outside but not *too* far outside what would be reasonable for you to ask at your specific stage. Clearly you won't get a high valuation unless you ask for it. So you do need to ask for a relatively high valuation, but you need to have a clue about what a typical valuation would be and what a ridiculously high valuation would be for your company. It's certainly an indication of how "money-raising savvy" somebody is. But even if they are money-raising savvy, it doesn't mean that they're going to be successful in the other aspects of the business, or even that they're even going to be a good investment to make. It's basically just another factor to add into the mix.

What do you see as really helping to create value for early-stage companies as they try to grow quickly and establish themselves?

I think it very much depends upon the area that they're in. If you take a consumer play such as PlanetAll, for example, it is much more important to establish a regular user base. "Regular" in the sense of "frequent users," which is at that point more important than making money off of them. For a consumer play, this is much more important than strategic relationships you might have. If, for example, you come in and say, "We have a million people who use our service on a regular basis," then investors are going to pay attention to you. If you come in and say, "We have relationships with Compaq, Dell, and Microsoft, but we have only 5,200 people using our service," then nobody's going to pay attention to you at all. So, in that area, user base is more important. If you're talking about a technology company such as Silknet or Intelligent Digital for example, then having built technology which everybody around us—from analysts to potential customers to partners and competitors in the market—looks at and says, "Those guys really have something special," can give you a valuation in the hundreds of millions all by itself, even if you don't yet have a single customer. So, it is much more important in that situation to develop first-class technology.

What in particular should entrepreneurs be looking for in the funding sources themselves?

The most important thing is a good personal relationship with the partner who's going to be doing the investment and sitting on your board. If he or she is not somebody who you really feel like you can work well with, you shouldn't be taking money from him or her because it is going to lead to problems sometime in the future. Even if everything else is right, the whole deal can go sour if the personal connection just isn't there. Beyond that, look for someone who has expertise in the area in which you're doing business. Their firm should also have a portfolio of companies that can be of use to you. Do your own due diligence by asking the CEOs of other companies that they have funded what their experience has been. There are a few tiers of VC firms, so you want to get the best firm that you can attract. It is not rocket science for the entrepreneur—it's a numbers scheme and a networking game. Lastly, try to network through connections and referrals because, VCs know that something that comes in as a referral is usually much better on average than something which comes in purely over the transom.

You hear so much these days about capital being so easy to raise. Is this really true?

There is a ton of capital around, but it is still focused upon a relatively small percentage of the addressable universe. It still is extremely difficult to raise money from the better-known VC groups. If you're willing to work long and hard enough at fund raising, however, you can probably find someone willing to give you money. If you're a dot com, it's easier to raise money simply because you're a dot com. However, it takes a long time and often nobody will have heard of your VC, which is not a bad think, but not a good thing either. So it remains a difficult task to find money unless you have the connections or you've made money for a VC before. If you have either of those two, then you have no problem raising money these days as long as you have a halfway decent idea. But those are the people who are saying that it is easy, not the much larger majority of people who have neither of these two characteristics.

When a company is doing a first round of financing, how much should they be looking to raise? Should they be looking for enough to take them through a major point in their company's life span?

That's the way to think about it. What you want to do is think about the growth path of your business and map out decisive changes that you hope to make happen. If you just have a business plan, then your next step would be to have some kind of prototype developed so that you've got something to show. If you already have a prototype, then developing some strategic partnerships can be a decisive change. If you have a prototype and strategic partnerships, the actual launching of your business or the registering of several thousand users to your service would be a decisive change. You need to think about each step as removing one additional layer of risk from the whole proposition, thereby making the company that much more attractive to a VC who is naturally risk-averse.

It's interesting to hear you say that, because one of the things that's often said is that an entrepreneur should have some sort of funding strategy. How important is it to have your funding strategy planned out a couple rounds in advance?

I think it's kind of like the financial section of a business plan: you plot out the projected financials in quite a bit of detail, but the one thing you're certain of is that they are going to change. That's the same way it is for your funding strategy as well. But there's a great deal of benefit in putting together the financial section because it forces you to think about the details and the essence of your business model. If you haven't been through that exercise, then you are essentially flying blind. Whereas if you have been through it, then you're adjusting a model to reality as things change and develop. The same applies to having a funding strategy.

STEPHEN ANDRIOLE
Safeguard Scientifics, Inc.

Steve Andriole has been with Safeguard since 1997. His main responsibilities include overall strategic vision with the aim of keeping Safeguard's acquisition strategy well ahead of the technology curve. Steve works closely with Safeguard's partner companies to keep them aligned with technology market trends. Previously, Steve was the Chief Technology Officer (CTO) and Senior Vice President for Technology Strategy at CIGNA Corporation. He was also the director of the Cybernetics Technology Office at the Defense Advanced Research Projects Agency (ARPA), and the founder of International Information Systems. Steve is listed in numerous "Who's Who" directories, the recipient of the U.S. Department of Defense Meritorious Service Award, is a Charter Member of the U.S. Senior Executive Service (SES), and the recipient of the Information Technology Exhibitions & Conferences (ITEC) Association's Lifetime Achievement Award in Information Technology, among other professional awards.

Safeguard's public partner companies include Cambridge Technology Partners, ChromaVision Medical Systems, Compucom Systems, Diamond Technology Partners, DocuCorp International, emerge Interactive, Internet

Capital Group, LifeF/X, OAO Technology Solutions, Pac-West Telecomm, Sanchez Computer Associates, Tangram Enterprise Solutions, US Interactive, and USDATA. Safeguard's private partner companies include 4anything.com, AgWeb.com, aligne, Arista Knowledge Systems, Extant, fob.com, Garage.com, HoopsTV.com, iMedium, Integrated Visions, Intellisource, Kanbay, MegaSystems, Multi-Gen-Paradigm, NexTone Communications, Nextron Communications, Opus360, QuestOne Decision Sciences, PrivaSeek, RealTIME Media, Redleaf Group, SOTAS, TechSpace, Vitts Networks, Whisper Communications, Who? Vision Systems, and XL Vision. Safeguard has also invested in venture funds including Cambridge Technology Capital, EnerTech Capital, Invemed Catalyst Fund, Pennsylvania Early Stage Partners, SCP Private Equity, Safeguard International Fund, and TL Ventures.

What are the important criteria when it comes to IT investing?

Information technology investment criteria come in several shapes and forms, but there at least four clusters that come to mind: the technology, the financial terms, the management team, the sales and marketing plan.

What are the questions you ask companies that you may be interested in investing in?

What's the technology trend you're riding? Why is it so hot? Are there any infrastructure implications to your products or services? Are there any unusual budget cycle opportunities or constraints to sales? Can you quantify the business benefits of your products and services? Does your product/service require buyers to change process or culture? Does your product or service represent a full solution to a real problem? Is there more than one way to win? What are your contingency plans? What's your horizontal strength? What's your vertical plan? What does the industry think of the product/service area and your company? How do you plan to market and sell? Who are your partners? Are your products/services in the political "sweet spot" of target buyers? What are your plans to recruit and retain talent? How would you differentiate your product/service from the competitions? What's your experience and track record in the sector? Have you developed effective marketing and communications materials?

What are the things that venture capitalists inspect prior to making an investment?

There are at least 15 things that they inspect prior to making an investment as well as on a continuous basis after the investments have been made:

1. Products and services that are on the right technology/market trends trajectory
2. Products and services that have the right infrastructure story
3. Products and services that sell clearly into budget cycles and budget lines

4.Products and services whose impact can be measured quantitatively

5.Products and services that do not require fundamental changes in how people behave or major changes in organizational or corporate culture

6.Products and services that represent total, end-to-end "solutions"

7.Products and services that have multiple "default" exits

8.Products, services, and companies that have clear horizontal and vertical strategies

9.Products and services that have high industry awareness recognition

10.Products, services and companies that have the right technology development, marketing, and channel alliances and partnerships

11.Products and services that are "politically correct"

12.Serious people and retention strategies in place or in the queue

13.Compelling "differentiation" stories

14.Executives who've "been there/done that"

15.Persuasive products and services "packaging" and communications: a damn good "elevator story"

How important is having the right technology?

This question assumes additional information. For example, the "right" technology assumes that the technology product or service is "hot" today and likely to remain so, or that it is about to become "hot" fast enough for you to catch the wave. It also assumes that, ideally, it's a high-margin area that a large number of prospective customers will need. In principle, for example, enterprise products and services would be better than small companies or little industry products and services.

How important are the infrastructure requirements?

Technology solutions that require large investments in existing communications and computing infrastructures—like more powerful desktops or more bandwidth—are more difficult to sell and deploy than those that ride on existing infrastructures. If IT managers have to spend lots more money to apply a company's product or service, they're less likely to do so if the choice is another similar product or service that requires little or no additional investments. A quick example: in order to implement Oracle's enterprise financial system, users have to first install the Oracle data base engine. If the user's current data base organization is DB2, Sybase, Informix, or MS SQL Server, then the move to Oracle is likely to be complicated and expensive. Peoplesoft's financial management system runs on any database—put another way, Peoplesoft's system requires less infrastructure modifications than Oracle's.

How important is it that the product or service fills the need of a major upcoming trend?

It's easier to sell into a new or growing budget cycle than into an older or shrinking one. As sales professionals have known for years, it's tough to sell at the end of the fiscal year. In order to make sales in November or December you have to get creative, often offering to defer billing until budgets get renewed. Another aspect of the budget cycle worth noting is the identification of "protected" budget lines, the lines for products and services that just about everyone agrees they need. Today, e-commerce projects are often considered "protected."

What sort of impact does a company's product/service need to have on the marketplace for it to be successful?

If a product's or service's impact can't be quantified, then one has to rely upon anecdotes to persuade prospective customers that the product or service is worth buying. But if impact *can* be quantified, then it can be compared against some baseline or current performance level. Clearly, if quantitative impact is huge—for example, reducing development costs by 40 percent or increasing communications by 30 percent—then it's easy to persuade customers to at least pilot a product or service. Ideally, impact reduces some form of pain, so to speak, though at times the impact of "vitamin pills" can be appealing. Quantitative impact also helps differentiate products and services. If a product or service requires organizations to dramatically change the way they solve problems or the corporate cultures in which they work, then the product or service will be relatively difficult to sell. Conversely, if a product or service can flourish within existing processes and cultures, it will be that much easier for organizations to adopt, and therefore easier for your company to sell. The best example here is the relatively slow adoption of groupware or "collaborative computing." Those who sell groupware products and services assume that organizations will want to share information and collaborate, even if the organization is by nature non-collaborative. Today, knowledge management is suffering the same fate: Gurus are selling group problem-solving and solutions repositories when organizations may or may not have large appetites for sharing.

Does your product/service need to address a complex problem in the marketplace?

Increasingly, the market is looking for integrated solutions to broad, complex problems. While it's great to sell personal computers, it's better to sell personal computers, asset management systems, break-and-fix support, *and* desktop management strategies. Why? Because clients need all of these services and must often work with multiple vendors. It's just plain easier—and often more cost-effective—to work with fewer vendors. And sometimes one strategic partner represents the best integrated solution. The newest breed of consultant is the solutions integrator, which purports to provide end-to-end support for whatever IT problems clients might have.

How important is it to have multiple paths to success?

Since not all deals work perfectly, it's nice when there are multiple paths to success. If a company is selling a vertical solution that can relatively easily move to another vertical industry, then there's contingency built into the plan. If a horizontal technology product can go vertical pretty easily, that's a good default. The point is simple: If a company's product or service is horizontally and vertically flexible, extensible, and adaptive, it stands a better chance for surviving unpredictable shifts in the competitive marketplace.

How important are horizontal and vertical strengths?

Microsoft is the quintessential horizontal technology company: It sells software to anyone and everyone, regardless of industry. But there are companies that sell only to specific industries, like insurance companies, banks, or pharmaceuticals. And there are companies, like IBM and many of the larger consulting and systems integration companies, that sell horizontally *and* vertically, with "practices" that specialize in multiple industries. The best products and services are those that have compelling horizontal and vertical stories, since customers want to hear about industry-specific solutions or solutions that worked under similar circumstances, like those of a competitor. Without a good vertical story, it will become more and more difficult to make horizontal sales.

Which industries are the best to attack with a new product or service?

If no one's ever heard of the product or service you represent, then you have a dual sales job ahead of you. First, you have to educate your audience and explain who you are and what you do; then, you have to persuade them about the value of your specific products and/or services. While there are sometimes huge opportunities to create brand-new awareness and become a market trendsetter in the process, it's often easier to sell into an area that already has high industry recognition. Perhaps the most obvious validation is from the conventional industry analysts, like Gartner, Meta, Giga, and Forrester. If a technology product or service is unknown to this community, then companies have to spend their own money to create awareness before they make a sale. Companies should also understand how to play the awareness game, how to work the analysts, and how to get into the upper right-hand quadrant of the magic analyst matrix.

What sort of impact can partnerships have?

It's getting harder and harder for companies to go it alone. Given trends in solutions integration, outsourcing, and the pace of technology change, it is especially incumbent upon new companies to form the right channel partnerships and alliances. While direct sales and marketing can often work extremely well, it helps to have the right friends in the right places saying the right things about your products and services. Relationships with the management and technology consulting companies, the systems integrators and the support vendors can extend a company's reach by orders of magnitude. Companies unaware of this reach are likely to miss important channel opportunities.

How do you decide if a company is attacking a good market opportunity?

It's difficult to convince conservative enterprise buyers of IT products and services to adopt something new. No one wants to live on the "bleeding edge." Many IT managers will not risk their careers on what they perceive as risky adventures, even if the "risky" product or service might really solve some tough problems. Buyers also want products and services that will ease real pain. While "vitamin pills" are nice to have, "painkillers" are essential. Reducing costs and staff, measurably improving processes, and improving poor service levels are painkillers that make buyers look smart. This is a good place to be—and to invest.

How important is it for new IT ventures to find the right people?

The IT labor shortage is real and likely to get worse. In fact, finding talented professionals to staff product and service companies is emerging as perhaps the most important challenge facing companies in all stages of development. Companies that have identified employee recruitment and retention as core competencies are more likely to survive and grow than those that still recruit and retain the old-fashioned way. Creative solutions to this problem are no longer nice to have, but a necessity. Creative recruitment and retention strategies are no longer vitamin pills—they are painkillers.

The key here is to see the right mix of technological prowess and management seniority to develop and deliver a successful product or service. Ideally, the management team has been there and done that, and is mature enough to deal with all varieties of unpredictable events and conditions. There are other ideal prerequisites: experience in the target horizontal and/or vertical industry, the right channel connections, the ability to recruit and retain talented personnel, the ability to work industry analysts, communicate and sell. To this list we might all add a number of qualities, but the key is to find experienced entrepreneurs knowing full well that past success is not necessarily a predictor of future success.

How important is it for a new company to differentiate themselves from other competitors in the marketplace?

If a company cannot clearly and articulately define its differentiation in the marketplace, then a large red flag should be raised about the company's ability to penetrate a competitive market. Differentiation is critical to success. While not every differentiation argument is fully formed when a company is first organizing itself, the proverbial "elevator story" better be at least coherent from day one. The best differentiation stories, of course, directly address the uniqueness, cost-effectiveness, and power of the new product or service.

While it may seem a little strange to acknowledge the primacy of style over substance and form over content, the reality is that style, form, and sizzle sell. Product and service descriptions and promotional materials should read well and look good, and those who present these materials should be professional, articulate, and sincere. Companies that fail to appreciate the importance of form, content, and sizzle will have harder climbs than those who embrace and exploit this reality.

What are the questions you pose to potential new or existing companies you may wish to invest in?

1.What's the technology trend you're riding?
2.How big and pained is the market?
3.How do you differentiate your product or service from the competition?
4.Are there infrastructure implications to the implementation of your product or service?
5.Does your product or service require buyers to change their internal processes or culture?
6.What are your horizontal strength and your vertical plan?
7.Is there industry awareness of your product or service?
8.Why is management capable?
9.What's the likely quantitative benefit of your product or service?
10.What's the sales and marketing plan?

What are the major areas you look at when deciding if you are going to invest?

At Safeguard Scientifics, Inc. we look at four major criteria clusters: market size and trajectory, differentiation in the marketplace, margin potential, and management. If we were forced to select just four, these would constitute our list, though we'd try to get a relatively large ownership percentage as well. We monitor trends in six areas to determine which domains make the most sense. We track developments in e-commerce, enterprise applications, infrastructure, platforms, acquisition strategies, and the overall financial volatility of the marketplace as well as consolidation trends.

MARC BENSON
Mid-Atlantic Venture Funds

Marc Benson began his career with AMF Incorporated, where he was responsible for finance, sales, marketing, and international functions. He has more than 30 years venture capital experience and was the recipient of Greater Philadelphia Venture Group's Blair L. Thomas Memorial Venture Award for career achievement in venture capital. Marc is the partner in charge of MAVF's Virginia office, and is a Vice-President of the general partners of the second and third funds.

MAVF portfolio companies include Advanced Software Applications, BDS, CALAN, Cema Technologies, Innovative Solutions & Support, Hurwitz Group, LockStar, Mesa Systems Guild, MicroE, Midas Vision Systems, Net Balance, NexTone Communications, Net2000 Communications, NxtWave Communications, Quadrant International, Ravisent Technologies, Response Networks, Scoreboard Wireless, Softrax, Visual Networks, Wisor Telecom, Xycom Holdings, Cendex, Frandata, MindLever.com, Para-Protect Services, Sprockets.com, TechTrader, Versient.com, womenCONNECT.com, Access Health, Interscope Technologies, Medtrex, National Packaging Systems, Quality Packaging Systems, Sequoia Software, UltraCision, U.S. Physicians, Axicon

Technologies, Elastomeric Technologies, Integrated Chipware, Metech, Quantum Epitaxial Designs, Turtle Beach Systems, Storeroom Solutions, Anytime Access, Allegheny Child Care Academy, Faith Mountain Company, and TDJ Group.

Explain to me a little bit why you think the venture capital world has received so much attention lately.

Well, it is perceived by some as a quick way to riches given the events that have occurred in the industry over the last four or five years. However, I think that the country has become much more entrepreneurial in nature. There are a lot of folks who have great ideas, great technology, good management teams, and can build successful enterprises in part because the VCs provide them with the capital to do so.

What is the most exciting part of what you do?

For me, it's watching people turn dreams into miracles. Building a small business is a very hard thing to do. It requires incredible commitment, energy, time, and enthusiasm, and the folks we back have those things.

How did you end up in the venture capital world?

I started out in the corporate world after college and spent 12 years with a Fortune 1000 company. I watched its demise—which was primarily due to poor management, poor motivation, and backward thinking—and decided I didn't want to work for a corporation anymore. I found a business that we were able to buy out in 1987; we took on venture capital and went the entrepreneurial route. In the early, days when venture capital was certainly not what it is today, we bought the company, turned it around, and sold it to a much larger multi-national company. The guys who had backed me were looking for a third operating partner at the time, so they asked me to join them after the sale of my company…and I did.

How was the process of raising the capital then different than it is now?

There was a lot less of it around back then and it was harder to get. It was also a lot more expensive. There was much more discipline in those days than there is today. Venture capitalists tended to stay with you longer. They weren't as willing to accept the losses and move on as they are today. In a lot of cases today, you get one shot at the brass ring, and if you don't get it, the VCs move on to their winners. The VCs when I did my deal 13 years ago were more inclined to stay with the companies for a longer period of time and help you through the difficult periods— which is not to say that some of them don't do that today as well. It was just more prevalent then than it is now. There wasn't nearly as much money around to put to work. On the other hand, I think that there weren't as many smart people in the business then as there are today.

Take me through a typical day for you now on the VC side of things.

A typical Monday would include a partner's meeting in the morning, two deal reviews in the afternoon, and incessant phone calls with portfolio CEOs and people who are looking for capital. I also spend a considerable amount of time reviewing due diligence with associates on particular deals. Tuesday might involve three deal review meetings where we have teams come in for a couple of hours and make presentations and an entrepreneurial gathering in the evening. Once again, the phone rings incessantly. It seems that for every dollar of venture capital available there are four people trying to get it—which is a good thing. Wednesday, I might sit on a breakfast panel and give a talk on raising venture capital for an early-stage company and attend a couple of board meetings, and then spend the rest of the day returning phone calls and reviewing business plans. The rest of the week is basically a combination of the foregoing.

Tell me a little bit about the investment philosophy of Mid-Atlantic Venture Funds and how you differentiate yourself from other venture capital firms.

It's becoming increasingly difficult to differentiate, but we've certainly been around a very long time in relative terms. Mid Atlantic (formerly NEPA Venture Funds) was formed in 1984, which, by today's standards, is a long time. We're currently in the process of raising our fourth fund, and we've made about 65 investments to date. We tend to be generalists in nature, and we've always been very seed-

and early-stage focused. We try to be the first institutional capital in the deals that we do. Historical revenues are not important to us. Our focus is on the management team. Because we're generalists, it's difficult to be an expert in every technology or every science. In fact, it's impossible. Our approach is to first focus on the CEO and his or her team. We then spend an inordinate amount of time delving into their backgrounds to ascertain that they have in fact achieved the things that they say they have. We don't back CEOs, for example, who come from the telecom industry and want to open up pizza parlors; we back people who have been in the industries that they are proposing to serve with a new company. We back CEOs who understand the customer needs, the competitive dynamics, the pricing models, and CEOs who have developed a competitive strategic advantage that they can execute. Most typically, the CEOs who we back have, in some form or another, been involved in the sales and marketing functions of the industries that they're going to serve. It doesn't mean that they don't have to have really good technologists on the team, but we are firm believers that commercializing good technology is more difficult that developing it.

Tell me a little about what role you feel venture capitalists in general have played in terms of structuring the Internet economy.

Well, this may be a self-serving comment, but I think that the access to the venture capital has essentially enabled it. Ultimately, there have been a lot of failures as well as successes, but the capital has provided the wherewithal to experiment with what works on the Internet. Without it, the Internet would not be nearly as far along or as mature as it is today. The capital intensity needed to reach the volume of customers that are required could not be done with angel financing and private savings. You had to have access to huge sums of capital, and the members of the VC community were the ones most willing to provide it. That's changed now. For example, now there are lots of corporate venture capital funds. Everybody is in the venture business today, so capital is pretty readily available. In this kind of a cyclical industry, that will come back at some point and manifest itself in the form of lower returns. It hasn't happened yet, but it will happen at some point. Ultimately times like these lead to higher prices being paid for less attractive opportunities, and at some point that comes back in the form of lower returns.

Tell me a little bit about some of your recent investments in Internet and technology companies.

Well, we have done a number of business-to-business deals. We don't have the capital to get involved in the business-to-consumer market, although we invested fairly early on with a community content deal that has not worked out as we expected. Obviously, I won't identify the company, but it turned out to be far more capital-intensive than we ever imagined, so we've moved away from content and community and tried to move into more infrastructure and transactional-based business-to-business companies. We feel these types of companies have tremendous recurring value if you can aggregate industry information and bring industry buyers and sellers to a single site.

Give me some specifics on a particular deal that has progressed quicker than you anticipated.

We invested in a company that was backed by a CEO who came out of the travel industry. For many years, he had provided travel and housing services to trade associations for their annual industry gatherings. He decided that he had enough contacts and could bring together enough people in order to build a site which would aggregate buyers and sellers of packaging machinery equipment. And, in the matter of just the few months since funding, he has managed to acquire some 350 customers and is generating healthy revenues—certainly not profitable, but generating healthy and growing revenues. Obviously, the market appreciates what he's done.

What do you think are some of the best business-to-business opportunities still waiting to be capitalized upon?

If you look at the analysts reports, the whole notion of dis-intermediating business-to-business commerce transaction is very attractive because of the amount of capital, time, and energy that can be saved. We are trying to focus on finding those kinds of deals, but so is everyone else.

How do you decide which deals interest you, given the size of your fund?

One of the things that we did early on was to address smaller markets that were more easily definable and more easily reachable but had limited scalability. We did this because we were concerned about the amount of capital that would be required to get a company to a positive cash flow status. We have found now that those business models, while they can work, don't provide the kinds of returns or haven't historically provided the kinds of returns that investors in venture capital funds want to see. Now, we prefer to take bigger slices of first-round investments in companies that are addressing bigger markets, but which are still led by the same kinds of management talent that we have always backed. We know that if we can get through those first milestones in addressing huge markets with innovative technologies that have not yet been attacked, we can almost always raise the capital, given the current investment climate, to get these companies through their second- and third-round funding needs. We're much more amenable to taking on those kinds of companies than we were, say, five or seven years ago.

You mentioned an interesting point about giving them enough cash to last through a certain milestone. When do you expect them to become cash flow positive?

There's a lot more art than science to that equation. We look at the assumptions and spend a fair amount of time scrubbing the financials. But, at the end of the day, we are really basing it on an instinct about whether this team understands the marketplace that they're going to serve and understands the dynamics that are required to become successful. And we almost always assume that their revenues will be half of what they think and their costs will be twice as much. When you tell them that, they often become offended, at least until it happens. Seriously, once we get to what we think they believe are realistic projections, we cut them in half and we double the expenses just to see what it looks like.

For a company going out and looking to raise a first round of capital, is there a specific milestone that it should be looking to achieve in order to identify the amount of funding they need?

From a macro standpoint, we sort of look at it as a "risk pyramid." The first-round guys take the technology risk, the market risk, and the execution risk—and they get rewarded for that because they pay lower valuations, relatively speaking. There's obviously a much greater chance of failure with companies at this stage. Before we go out for a second round, we like to eliminate the technology risk by getting a product into beta and making sure it works. At this point, with the technology risk significantly reduced, you are left with the market and execution risks. The second-round guys will bet on market and execution. They'll do their due diligence and spend some time trying to figure out whether the market is what the company represents it to be, and, if convinced, they'll invest in that round. The third-round guys also want the market risk largely eliminated. They want to bet on execution, because by that time, you've proven that there is a customer for your product and that your product works. The third-round guy is essentially betting that the company is going to be able to do it better than anybody else is. There is a whole host of milestones that fall within those three major categories, but as we think about going from the first to the second round, we want to make sure that we have done everything possible to take the technology risk out of the equation. And we never invest so much that we can't do the second round ourselves, just in case we need to provide capital, because the company hasn't quite gotten to where they thought they were going to get.

How important is it for an Internet-based company to have some sort of proprietary technology?

It's important but not critical in my estimation. Capital and execution are much more important than technology. Entrepreneurs will often come in and tell us that they have applied for a patent on some arcane technology. In software, which is the driver of all this, there are a lots of ways around every patent. If you're starting a biotechnology company, it's a different story. We spend very little time on intellectual property value and much more time on what the market for the product is, who wants it, and what they are willing to pay for it.

What criteria do you use when you are looking to value an Internet or technology business?

That's a complex question but one that we run up against every single day. We were talking amongst ourselves recently, because in the course of the last two days we had one company that waltzed in here with a business plan and a halfway team that was looking for a $75 million pre-money valuation on a company with no revenues and no customers. A second company, also a dot com and also with no revenues, wanted $50 million. We told them both that we were not the appropriate investors for them at those kinds of valuation expectations, and while I might have believed a few years ago that they would never get what they were looking for, I am no longer so sure. On the other hand, our firm still believes that valuation discipline has a place among all this euphoria. At some point, as I mentioned earlier, the tide will turn and people will be getting out of deals at lower prices than which they got in—we don't want to find ourselves in that situation. If you come in with an early-stage team who's addressing a huge market, an innovative strategy, a clear understanding of the competitive dynamics, a seasoned CEO and sales team, but has no revenues and no customers, you're probably in the $5 to $10 million pre-money range. If you have less than that, you're obviously going to be in a lower pre-money valuation category.

One of the things that we're able to provide our companies with is access to a growing number of venture banks that are located in this region of the country. They include Silicon Valley Bank, Imperial, and PNC Venture Bank. The funding that these institutions make available allows us to leverage our money with relatively inexpensive bank debt. So if a company needs $5 million and wants a $10 million pre-money valuation, we can say to that company, "Look, we'll give you the $3 million, and our being in the deal will allow the bank to put another $1.5 to $2 million of working capital. At a pre-money valuation of $6 million, the dilution is no greater than if you were taking the entire $5 million in equity." So we use that bank leverage to our benefit to try to keep valuations within a disciplined range.

It's interesting that you mentioned the new types of banks that are offering entrepreneurs debt financing never before available. How often do you use them in your deals?

We use them now on virtually every deal.

Why do you look to do that?

It allows our money to go a lot further than it would without the bank, put two or three additional milestones behind us, and get an extra six months of working capital before we have to decide that it makes sense to go out and raise another round. This also allows us to get a higher valuation, as the company is ostensibly making an additional six months of progress. And it also gives us more time to figure out whether this was a good investment or not.

When an entrepreneur is raising their first round of capital, should they be looking to raise a year's worth of cash?

I think that is absolutely the correct approach. Definitely not less. Fund raising is a very time-consuming effort, and it takes a lot of the CEO's energy and commitment out of his or her ability to run a business. We don't like to see a deal that isn't funded at least 12 months and preferably 18 months out, and that doesn't even include the bank debt.

Tell me about the role that you play when you make an investment in a company.

Well, it has always been our view that being the first institutional investor in a deal, we have a pretty significant amount of influence on the composition of the overall deal, co-investors, and terms. We try very hard to build a constructive relationship with the management team and to become the CEO's most trusted confidant. We are not what you would call a "heavy hands-on" investor. Some VCs tend to be very hands-on—it just depends on each firm's philosophy. Our belief is that if we have to run the companies we've backed, we've obviously invested in the wrong people. For example, we want to be there to help them with the hiring process, because we've interviewed thousands of people, know good interview techniques, and know how to get the right people. In addition, we play a large part with additional fund raising by introducing them to our contacts with later-stage investors and, ultimately, the investment banking community. We also have contacts in the accounting, banking, and legal communities that are often of help. We do not add that much value in the marketing and sales strategy of a company because it's not where our expertise lies.

Tell me about where you see the Internet developing in the next five to ten years.

That's one of those questions that I only wish I knew the answer to. I think the power of that medium is just beyond our comprehension today. I don't know where it will go, but I wish I did. In the short term, we shall see a lot of value in dis-intermediation—companies like Priceline.com. We're looking exactly for those kinds of opportunities. But where it ultimately goes, it is anyone's guess.

What do you feel are some of the main factors that will shape the Internet marketplace?

I think bandwidth is one of the biggest ones. It seems like every time there are increases in bandwidth, there are increases in the ability to use it up. We do a lot in telecom because we think that telecommunications is ultimately the key in terms of how that information will get from point to point with as little delay and as much reliability as possible. Right now, however, the limitation is bandwidth. Ultimately, you'll be able to watch a movie on your PC – although I guess you can already do that now if you've got the pipe for it. As the bandwidth constraints that exist today get reduced and removed over the next two or three years, I think it will just add immensely to the power of what the Internet can do.

What creates value for an early-stage Internet or technology company? Is it actually getting users, customers, revenues, partnerships, or something else?

I think it's all of the above. Users obviously are important, you've got to get eyeballs to your site. If you have a model that allows for the immediate generation of some revenues, even though they may not be profitable revenues, I think that it proves that there's a business model there that might work. It seems to me and to our firm that the fundamentals aren't all *that* different than they have been historically. Ultimately, you have to be able to make money at this because you can't keep using other people's money. You've got to provide a return at some point. But what's happened, I think, is that people have seen the ultimate power of what the Internet can do, and are much more patient in terms of spending money to acquire customers and building the infrastructure that will eventually result in the generation of positive cash flow. It costs money to put the servers and the pipes in; we understand that. Just show us growth. Show us top-line growth. We are not as concerned about bottom-line growth at this point. That seems to be the view of the world. At some point, that will come around and Internet companies—just like every other company in the history of the world—will have to make money.

What does it take to have continued success raising capital from round to round? Is it basically just hitting the milestones that you identified with your original capital source?

I think that right now everybody is focused on top-line growth and eyeball growth, the belief being that if you can build that, you'll ultimately reach the turning point. Once you've hit that, it can become a pretty profitable model.

What sort of effect do you think a market crash would have on the venture landscape?

It will be significant. It happened in 1987 and valuations plummeted. The window on the public market shuts down and all of that cash that was available through selling equities to the public markets dries up. When that happens, it creates a situation where the public markets can no longer bail you out, and private equity has to do it. Therefore, private equity becomes tighter because it's fueled by the profits of the public markets and it's a vicious circle. Capital will be much harder to raise both from the venture perspective and the entrepreneurial perspective and it will become much more expensive. And, in my estimation, it will not be an unhealthy thing. I mean, the excesses are pretty significant today.

Do you think it's set to happen shortly?

I have no idea. I have a partner who would tell you it could happen any day now. He says, "I've correctly predicted zero of the last eight recessions," or something like that. Ultimately, it will happen. I have no idea when. I think the trick, and I said this early on, is to build businesses that are able to sustain themselves even in a market correction. Businesses that ultimately have a path to sustainable positive cash flow and teams that know how to manage in times that aren't quite as good as they are today are the ones that will succeed. The one thing we have learned is that if you build value, ultimately the exit always takes care of itself in one form or another.

Tell me about some companies that aren't necessarily in your portfolio that you admire.

I admire Amazon.com because Jeff Bezos did it before anybody else succeeded, and he's been rewarded for it. I admire companies like Priceline, Ariba, Commerce One, ICG, and CMGI as well. I admire the people who are in the telecom space who recognized early on that Internet and data would drive their futures. The list just goes on and on and on.

How will the advent of the Internet and technology in foreign countries affect US-based dot coms?

More opportunities, it's as simple as that.

Do you think we'll see a lot more of the US-based dot coms going overseas?

I think we already have. Companies like Benchmark and CMGI are doing it now, and Patricoff has been doing it for years already. But now the rest of them are following. Draper Fisher is talking about going overseas. Benchmark is opening an office in London. It's happening all around.

How different is it to build an Internet or technology business internationally?

The building of businesses isn't all that different. I think, from a regulatory perspective, it might be slightly different: the more underdeveloped nations and developing nations that these folks go into, the higher the risk. If you go to Central Europe—France, Italy, the UK—where they do business much like we do, it'll probably be a gold mine for the next five or six years. If you go to Russia and the former communist countries, I think it's still very dangerous.

What sort of role do you play in determining whether the company is ready to go public or should be sold?

Basically, we are an adviser and screener. We obviously take part in the investment banking meetings, for example. If it's a public offering or sale, we take part in the negotiations as well. At the end of the day, however, if we've gotten to the point where real value has been created, we are typically not in a control position. Our CEOs know going in that we have to get out at some point. They understand that. They're not building lifestyle businesses here. They're building companies that they ultimately hope will provide them with liquidity, and the whole process tends to be very much a team effort. But at the end of the day, we still view it as their company and they take the lead in those things. We really act as helpers and counselors.

How important is it for the early-stage companies to begin developing actual revenues, and at what point should they be looking to be profitable?

Well, it's a lot less important than it was five or ten years ago. It is our opinion, however, that it is still very important. We don't like to do deals where we can't see revenues 12 months out. We don't mind doing the prototype and going through the beta phase and funding that, but we generally like to see how the company will begin generating revenues 12 months or so from date of investment.

How do you find out about most of the companies that you're investing?

We have an incredible referral network. We've been around a very long time, and find most of our deals from lawyers, accountants, bankers, deal-finders, brokers and former CEOs who we know. I would guess that about 150-200 deals a month come through this office. We have two full-time associates who screen plans, and we make an effort to meet with as many teams as possible. The deal flow is incredible.

With so many business plans coming through, what are you really looking for? What catches your eye?

Team, experience, market, and common sense. Does this proposal pass the common sense test? Is this something that's been engineered in someone's basement and spammed to every venture capitalist, or is it founded on real-world experience and a real-market need? You get to the point where you can get a pretty good sense of whether the deal is worth pursuing after a 10-minute review of the business plan.

What are you looking at specifically in business plans that you are interested in?

Well, the financial projections we discount very heavily because they all come in with numbers that they will mostly likely never achieve, particularly in the early years of a company's development. In 60 or so deals, we had one company that ever made its numbers from day one. Which is not to say that we haven't had some companies that have been enormously successful—we have. But it took them longer and cost them more than they thought it was going to. We look very closely at their competitive strategies. What's the differentiation between this company and every other one out there? What is the marketplace? Who are the customers and why will they buy? If someone can articulate those things in a business plan, then you sit up and take notice. At that point, you think that you're reading a plan from a team who truly understands what it is they're trying to accomplish and, more important, how they are going to do it.

Tell me how you keep on top of everything that's changing.

We don't keep on top of everything that's changing. But one thing that *doesn't* change is the values and experience of people. You can always make a quick first judgment in terms of the people who are proposing that you invest in them. On the technology side, we understand technologies by hiring professionals to do it for us. There are all kinds of telecom and Internet experts around, and we've gotten to know and trust some of them. We have contacts in the companies we've backed and we talk to existing CEOs and other technology folks. There is a host of ways to find out if what is being proposed is realistic.

How far along does an entrepreneur need to be in his or her idea to be ready for funding?

He doesn't need to be very far along at all. We'd like to see him have put together a well-structured business plan. That's important to us because it's an indication of how he thinks. But we've done many deals where there was no product and no customers.

When you're doing that, you're obviously looking at the person, their experience, and other things, such as the size of the market. What are some of the specifics that really give you insight into whether an entrepreneur is "backable?"

I think it goes back to the earlier comment. Does the idea pass the common sense test? Is there evidence of a market for it? Does he have a competitive strategy that differentiates him from the masses that are out there doing the same thing? Because in the Internet, if you've got an idea, 20 other people have it today as well. So what makes yours different? What experiences do you have that will allow you to get through the learning curve faster than the competitors? They're subtle clues, but there are enough of them that when you lump them all together, you get a pretty good sense of whether you're dealing with reality or whether you're dealing with fluff.

How easy is it for an Internet or tech startup to raise capital right now?

If the idea is any good, it's really easy. We turn down lots of deals that end up getting funded.

What's the best way for an entrepreneur to go about starting the funding process and looking for the right capital?

I think the best way is to go talk to one of the preeminent venture accountants, lawyers, or bankers, and get those folks to make referrals to some of the VCs. We get a tremendous amount of business plans sent to us, and it's not that we don't read them, but they don't get quite the level of attention that a highly regarded referral gets.

What should the entrepreneurs be looking for in the VC themselves in terms of conducting their own due diligence?

I always counsel entrepreneurs to ask for a list of all of the CEOs who the venture capitalists to whom they're talking have backed. If the VC won't give it to you, that tells you all you need to know. If she does give it to you, pick out half a dozen or more on the list and call them. With five or six simple questions, you can learn all that you need to know about this VC as a prospective partner. Some of those questions are: How long have you worked with these VCs? How well do you know them? What have they been like when times were good, and more important, when times were bad? What value did they bring to the investment? Do you trust them? If you were going to do it again, would you bring them as your key investor? These CEOs are a pretty independent bunch, and they are going to give their honest opinions. Having sat on that side of the table myself, I always counsel entrepreneurs that if you can't get that out of your prospective investor, then you'd better go find somebody else who will give it to you. These relationships tend to last a very long time and can have a huge impact on whether you ultimately succeed. Not to mention that having some fun along the way ought to be part of the deal.

What is the typical length of time you are in a deal for?

Historically, it's been three to seven years. It's shorter now, because you find out more quickly if the company has momentum or if it isn't going to make it. So now it's probably three to five years on average.

When do you feel that a company is not going to make it? What is it that turns the tide?

There is no single thing that tips you off to that. It's a compendium of events, missed numbers, inability to finalize beta contracts and initial customer orders, and people defections, among other things. It's just a whole host of things that don't go right. It usually takes the better part of a year to see that happen, but it becomes evident after a time. For VCs, the hardest part of the job is deciding when to stop funding because, as we all know, you can keep a company alive forever if you just keep putting money in it. The tough decision for us is when do you reach the conclusion that this one just isn't going to make it, and it's time to move on.

ROGER NOVAK
JACK BIDDLE
Novak Biddle Venture Partners

Roger Novak has over 20 years of experience as a venture capitalist, angel investor, investment banker, and operating principal. He was a founder and General Partner of Grotech Partners, where he was principally focused on information technology. Jack Biddle was CEO of Annapolis based InterCAP Graphics Systems from 1990 to 1995. Previously, Jack was a principal at the software focused merchant bank Vanguard Atlantic Ltd. where he focused on numerous venture deals.

Novak Biddle Venture Partners have invested in companies such as AnswerLogic, Blackboard, DiamondBack Vision, Engenia Software, Entevo Corporation, Giga Information Group, LifeMinders.com, Para-Protect Services, Paratek Microwave, Princeton Electronic Systems, Simplexity.com, Tantivy Communications, Telogy Networks, Torrent Systems, and Woodwind Communication Systems.

Tell me a little bit about your investment philosophy and how your fund got started.

Roger: We're an early stage fund and invest only in information technology. Jack Biddle and I formed it because we were concerned that there weren't enough top-quality true seed funds out there to help early-stage companies get started. We're usually the first institutional money in a company and we are unusual in the fact that we will even write a $50,000 or $100,000 check. I would say we are probably more technically oriented than a lot of the funds and most of the companies in our portfolio have a technology component. We're also really active in the companies we invest in.

Why is it that you like the seed-stage investments instead of later-stage companies?

Jack: Once a company is off and running and has some traction in the market they're going to be funded, it's just a question of by whom and at what price. Where we're investing we really make a difference from the beginning and that's what motivates both of us. I don't know how to write a symphony or build a supercomputer, but I do know how to be a patron to people who can. That's really our job—to be patrons of really talented people who otherwise wouldn't have a chance to do really great things. We've got some very significant companies in which now we have lots of other institutions fighting to get in on the follow-on rounds. In fact, many of our companies might have never existed unless we backed them. It's really satisfying to change history.

What are you looking for in these early-stage companies that helps you identify good opportunities?

Jack: If you look at our portfolio, you see exceptionally high IQ's attacking technically difficult problems. Their principal motivation is to change the world, not to get rich. They're also all in sexy markets. The other thing we look for in our entrepreneurs is people who have been successful at everything they've ever done in their lives. Because with the companies we fund, the original plan never works. It always has to get changed. That's what all of our good companies have in common.

Roger: We really want a unique proprietary advantage. I place a large emphasis on the market, particularly at the seed stage, because you can't predict who's going to win. But if we get any one of five initiatives right in a huge market, we'll probably make money. Basically we really want to see scalability. The other thing is, I think all of our entrepreneurs are pretty creative people. They have an innate ability to adjust as they see changes. Another emphasis is that we really want to have fun with our entrepreneurs.

How is your fund different than other seed-stage funds?

Roger: We set up our fund very differently than most other funds, although it is being copied now in various places, which I guess is the sincerest form of flattery. We went out and got sixty really bright and successful information technology entrepreneurs as our original investors in the fund. We then got together other institutions and groups to form our own version of a keiretsu. The idea was you could take a company and, within our group, finance it from seed all the way through. By having these big guys around from the beginning it makes it an easy sell to others later down the line. The strategy has worked very well so far.

Jack: We've had enormous returns just like everybody else has, but the companies we're backing have the potential to be making profits in the near-term. I think a vast majority of the deals we're seeing funded today are like Hollywood sets—they're being built for the public markets. There's nothing behind the facades and they're not real businesses. I think we're building valuable long-term businesses.

How important is it for a company that you're investing in to have some sort of proprietary technology?

Jack: I think our philosophy is a little different. We live in the most competitive world in history. Capital is essentially unlimited. As soon as somebody starts to generate monopoly profits, the venture guys are going to throw hundreds of millions of dollars to go after them. Even if the pioneer wins, it's not a real victory because they're not going to be able to make any money in the long-term. Competition always drives price towards cost eventually. So, long-term the only way to make money is to be a monopoly, and the only way to be a monopoly is to have something that's significant and that you can protect. The easiest monopoly today is technology, but you still have to build a mousetrap that can capture profits. Also, the world has changed a lot and I don't think people have realized that being first doesn't guarantee profitability anymore.

Tell me about a recent investment in a space that you like right now.

Jack: We invested in a company called Blackboard, which was founded by two 26 year-old kids who were clearly extremely intelligent and wanted to change the world. This wasn't about money. In fact, one of the founders taught high school before. These guys have been friends since they were 18 years old and went to American University together. One was the campaign manager for the other's successful campaign to be president of the school. After college, he taught junior high school in D.C. and had an epiphany that technology would make it possible for everybody to get a first-rate education. He had an idea to build a platform where any university's content could be brought online for distance learning. We funded them and the company now, less than two years old, has two million kids and 1700 institutions on this system. They are really going to be a huge company. What we liked about this deal was education. The VCs historically would not invest in education, because they didn't think there was any money there to be made. To Roger and me, education is going to be the next killer app. You have blue-collar families who make $40,000 a year able to scrimp and save and come up with between $6,000 to $10,000 to give their kid a college education. If people are willing to part with 25% of their pre-tax income for something, it clearly represents a fantastic market. When we backed them, no one was doing education. Now VCs are pouring money into education. But these kids have 170 people and have a real sustainable advantage.

When you work with entrepreneurs in early-stage companies, how much do you let them run with their ideas? What are the areas you are really adamant about?

Roger: The really good entrepreneurs are pretty honest people. They recognize if something's not working, and hopefully what we've done is build a relationship where they feel they can tell us it's not working and we can help them work through it. It's not like we're going to take them behind the woodshed and whip them. I would say that where we're toughest is really on valuation, not day-to-day matters once we have funded a company.

Jack: We're also especially tough on the first round of six or so hires. We'll turn down a lot of people because we are really trying to set a very high standard with regard to the quality of people. Mostly because each of these people will be hiring the next wave of people and you have to get it right from the start. If your first six or so hires are good ones, you're halfway finished.

Roger: The other thing is you don't see us taking 55% of the company in round one. We want the management to have a lot of ownership. You see a lot of people now putting a ton of money in the initial round and taking a 50% or 60% stake in the company. We think that doesn't work because it doesn't leave enough money on the table for both current and future employees.

What is the secret to valuing such early-stage companies?

Jack: It's like a riddle, but really very simple. In the later mezzanine-type rounds before an IPO the valuations are discounted to the public equivalents, so they'll be at a 60% or 70% discount to a publicly-traded comparable company. Right now in the middle rounds, the Series B and C rounds, it's simply supply and demand. In the early stage where we invest, in most cases if we don't fund them, they don't get funded. This being the case there is really not a lot of negotiation. It's not like the Series B and C rounds where if we don't offer a good enough valuation, there are ten or so other funds looking to do the deal and able to offer a higher valuation. So in early-stage investing, they're all pretty much at a $3 million pre-money valuation if it's a really good idea and they have a really good team. If it's kind of a risky opportunity then it might be $2 million pre-money valuation. If it's a good idea, they don't have a great team, and it's a risky opportunity then it can be a $1 million pre-money valuation. If they have a great idea, a great team, and are in a great market then it can get as high as a $5 million pre-money valuation.

Roger: The other thing to keep in mind is that we're not backing a lot of experienced entrepreneurs who have done this before. We're mostly backing engineers, people who've almost been there, or great people who never really had an opportunity.

Jack: There is really no exact way to come up with a valuation for early-stage companies. One of our portfolio companies once told us the "behind the scenes" story of their funding experience. We had a couple of meetings with them and on the last one, I asked the Company to leave the room. We decided we wanted to do it and five minutes later told them we would invest at a $3 million pre-money valuation. They accepted, and told us about another venture fund that had spent four weeks running the numbers and calculating all sorts of equations that came back with the same number.

Tell me about some of the specific developments you think are going to seriously alter the IT space.

Roger: We're seeing an increasing number of communications related deals and I would not be surprised to see 65% to 70% of the next fund being in communications related deals. If you look worldwide right now it is really the fastest growing industry. I think there's a limit to how many business-to-consumer things you can do right now.

What are some of the difficulties all technology companies are facing right now?

Roger: An area I think that's become increasingly important is the whole concept of human capital management. The key is identifying how you go about managing, getting, and retaining really good people. I think you will especially see a lot of movement from the big companies to the smaller ones.

What are some of the misconceptions that have developed regarding venture capitalists?

Jack: You are going to see stories on the front page of *Forbes* and *Fortune* in the next three years lambasting venture capitalists and saying that we perpetrated the biggest fraud in history because the area is so over-funded. It's getting sloppy and reckless at this point because of all the outlandish public valuations. When the public window closes, a majority of the new VCs are going to lose their shirts. I don't know whether it happens in six months or two years, but it's a cyclical business that everyone thinks they understand right now.

Why are there so many new faces getting into the venture capital world? All of a sudden it seems like everyone has a fund.

Jack: People ask us all the time how you get into the VC business. There's only one high probability way of doing it: get your BS from CalTech, your BA from Harvard, MIT, or Stanford, then go be a product manager at Hewlett Packard. Then you really have a good chance of getting into the business at the lowest level. The only other way is to get really rich and start your own fund.

Do you anticipate international dot com startups will pose significant competition to already established US dot coms?

Roger: Clearly in the mobile area they will, but in other areas I think we are so far ahead.

Jack: It's fashionable right now for all of the economic development types and the World Bank to talk about if they had venture capitalists, but VCs are only 5% of the reason we have developed so quickly. There has to be good education, the economy, the public markets, the culture of winning, and many other things for it to happen. The VCs are so predominant in the U.S. because all of this stuff is here.

It is interesting if you look at the rate of engineers specifically migrating to the U.S. from other countries. What sort of effect is this going to have?

Jack: The amazing part is that we're not just getting good ones, we're getting their geniuses. I really don't know how you develop a country with your top talent leaving.

When you're investing in these early-stage companies are you encouraging most of them to take on some sort of venture bank financing?

Jack: Absolutely. It just gives you a little more leverage in the deal. The money is available, and it's at a relatively low cost. The venture banks have a very interesting model—the truth is that they will invest in any deal that a good VC goes in on.

What are the main things you encourage your companies to stay focused on as they grow so quickly?

Roger: It really depends on what the natural ability of that entrepreneur is. Some people are really good at sales and marketing while others have more operations experience. We find ourselves spending a lot of time coaching in the areas they're not strong in.

Jack: Each company has their own list of things they have to execute on. If they do this, they win. If they don't do it, they lose. We have a company that's really pushing a state-of-the-art technology in video compression. What we've helped them realize is that they should focus everything they've got on recruiting Ph.D.-level mathematicians and engineers who can make this work, because if it works, it allows a Micrsoft or an Intel or a Real Networks to put everyone else out of business. So if this happens, they will get bought out for more money than they could have ever imagined and if it doesn't work it's completely irrelevant to what their plans are for the other stuff. So it started out as a broad plan, and we helped them identify the two or three things, the two or three relationships that it is all going to boil down to. If they do those things right, they will win. So now the whole company is focused on succeeding in those specific areas.

How do you handle it when one of your portfolio companies is not hitting their milestones?

Roger: You go back and try to decide if their targets were too high, if the model is no good, if the market is slow to develop, or if it is an execution issue. If it's an execution issue, then you begin to start thinking maybe it's time to sell the company. Then again, others may feel it needs more money. So you really try and quantify why it is you're not making it. This again goes back to the relationship that you forged along the way, because you don't want the entrepreneur to think every time he delivers bad news you're going to be annoyed. It just drives me crazy when someone from the new generation comes in and sits on these boards for big funds, having never built businesses themselves, and creates tension when every milestone is not hit.

NURI WISSA
Kestrel Venture Management

Nuri joined Kestrel (formerly Corning Venture Management) in 1989 after having been a member of Arthur Young & Company's Entrepreneurial Services Group, an organization focused on emerging businesses and venture capital firms. Nuri has served as a General Partner of five venture capital funds that have invested in more than 35 companies.

Kestrel Venture Management has invested in companies such as Cambridge Applied Systems, IntraServer Technology, Pixelvision, Progressive Technologies, Berkshire Wireless, Data Profit, Sensitech, Zentox, Applied Internet Technologies, Asset Sciences, ConneXus, Datacube, Keyfile, Personal Health Technologies, Residential Delivery Services, Web CT, USDATA, Global Telemedix, MassTrace, MedSafe, Autolines, iDolls, KaBloom, Kid Galaxy, Desktop Data, and Voicetek.

Tell me about your background and how you got into the venture capital business.

Following college I joined Arthur Young & Company in their entrepreneurial services group, which was focused on providing a full range of services for companies from zero to about $50 million in revenues. All of my clients were venture capital-backed companies and I found it much more interesting from their side than mine. I eventually left to join Corning Venture Management in 1988 and I have been involved directly in the venture capital business ever since.

Tell me about some of the investments that your firm has made so far in the Internet and technology space.

As you know, so many of the companies today have migrated toward some sort of Internet-or technology-based model. Even companies that we have had in our portfolio prior to the Internet have really adapted themselves to be more Internet-like companies. Companies that we're funding in this area include a company called Applied Internet Technologies, which provides graphics software for the apparel industry. It was actually a company that we backed originally in a non-Internet area that has completely changed their business model to capitalize on the capabilities provided by the Internet. We also invested in a company called Autolines, which is a brick and mortar automobile store that is now transitioning to the Internet and already getting a great deal of traffic on their site.

It sounds like a lot of your investments are in traditional brick and mortar companies that are finding ways to capitalize on the Internet in some fashion. What are some of the things that you're looking for in the investments you're making?

First and foremost are the people. It almost sounds like a cliché, however you really do not have anything at all without the right people. The key is to find driven, smart, and high integrity managers whose interests are aligned with ours. We're in the business of creating companies in which we can exit at a much greater value at some point in the future. We are not in the business of helping somebody build a company that his or her children will take over some day.

How do you feel your firm is different than some of the other venture firms in the similar space?

We've been around for quite a while and all of the senior investment professionals here have invested in bad times as well as good times. We've been through a number of cycles and there are not many people in this business today who remember the early nineties when you couldn't get anything funded. Fortunately, or unfortunately, we were operating in that period. We are also very good at establishing and maintaining a partnership with the management teams and our entrepreneurs. We firmly believe that unless that partnership is established and maintained, it reduces the chance for a successful outcome with the business. Hence, we only invest in companies in our region that we can get to within a car ride. We have invested in up to about eighty companies now and have really generated a wealth of experience.

How important is it for a startup to have some sort of proprietary technology? How much value do you place on that?

I think we put a great deal of value on that with a caveat that regardless of how proprietary or exclusive the technology is, if you don't have a management team to implement it and run with it it's not going to go anywhere. The reason that companies fail is not because they have bad technology—they have management teams that are unable to adapt to a change of environment. Even the best of technologies at some point are going to have to be enhanced, so you have to have a management team that's able to enhance that technology and react to the environment they're in at all times.

What are some of the industries right now that you find extremely attractive from an investment standpoint?

We're seeing a backlash now as the venture markets migrate more from business-to-consumer to business-to-business opportunities. I think where I see the real opportunities are in ways you can blend both the consumer side and the business side together. However, you have to be careful not to get too overly exposed in terms of the need for direct advertising and marketing dollars that compete with some of your other customers.

How important do you think profitability is going to be for Internet and technology companies, regardless of whether they're on the business-to-consumer or

business-to-business side over the next three to five years?

I think it's going to have to be very important. We're clearly going to see some backlash due to the disregard of earnings in the near future, especially for private medium-stage companies. If you look at what a company has to earn in order to absorb their acquisition costs of new customers, it is inevitable that these companies will have to start making money in the near future.   In all of the companies that we've invested, our goal is to make money. We are not looking for 5000% returns, however we want to see growth rates for the next twenty years and a profitable business model that works.

How much capital should a seed-stage company be looking to raise in their first round of funding?

Depends upon where they are in their fund raising and how quickly they need the cash. In many of our pure Internet-related deals we have put in short-term financing facilities leading up to a first round fund raising in order to tide them over. That money generally won't last more than a few months, and it's our understanding that we will bring in other folks to co-invest with us and then convert our money into that round. And then I would hope that a company could last six to twelve months until it needed to go out for another round of funding, but it all depends upon how quickly the company progresses.

Are you encouraging any of your early-stage companies to take on some sort of debt through venture banks in order to make their first round of funding last longer?

Most of our companies have some sort of venture-leasing facilities in place or have established a more traditional line of credit with a bank. We actually do this in most of our investments.

What do you think helps Internet and technology startups achieve value? Is it board members, partnerships, customers, a funding team, or other things along those lines?

Partnerships, customers, all of the above. The solid funding helps to get a solid team, which in turn helps to develop the partnerships, which help to get the customers. On the funding side for instance, in one of our companies we've been very fortunate to have a number of strategic investors that have given the company instant credibility.

Are strategic investments right for every company? What are the types of companies that they really make a difference with? A lot of times don't you see strategic partners entering the picture more so right before an IPO?

This is usually the case because their risk profile is different and they're not venture funds. They're not providing high-risk capital so they need more of a "sure investment," more of a known success. There are companies, however, that strategic investors don't make sense for at all. Where it doesn't make sense is if it blocks you as a company from doing business with other companies. An example is if you're going to end up having a strategic investor who is a customer of yours, and he has 20% of the market. If you form a partnership with him, it precludes you from working with the other 80% of the market because now you are seen as a competitor. That doesn't make a lot of sense, and there are lots of cases where this happens.

What is it that really catches your eye when you're looking at a business plan?

The first thing that I like to see is a large enough market that is going to be receptive to the technology or product. A market in which one is able to get good leverage for their dollars and a market that's defensible over a period of time. It is really important that once you discover a market, you find a way to exploit and protect it so that some big guy does not come along and take advantage of what you discovered. In fact, we've made investments like that where we've seen it happen. Let's say you create a consumer product, and come up with something like Wonder Cream 28. Regardless of how good your technology is, you're never going to have enough marketing dollars to compete against the likes of Johnson & Johnson and the other big consumer companies. You don't have enough power because you're unable to get or afford the shelf space in the supermarkets and you don't have the people to market it on a nationwide basis. You really have to find markets where you're just not going to get killed by larger, more established companies.

How do you think your background in terms of making investments in other industries helps you advise new Internet and technology ventures?

I think that there is a lot to be said for bringing a broader perspective to the table. There is also clearly a lot to be said nowadays for market specialization, and I think that we are now seeing this in our firm as well. I am now spending probably 80% of my time working with IT-and Internet-related companies where this wasn't the case even a couple of years ago.

What do you think are some of the biggest financial challenges that an early-stage company faces?

Leveraging their business model and getting the most bang for their buck. There is now a sense of urgency that has really never existed in terms of getting companies up and running as quickly as possible. There are some exceptions obviously but we really haven't ever seen management teams that have this sort of energy. In one of my portfolio companies the average age is about 27, and these people work incredible hours that you can't do when you're 45, at least not every day. They have an amazing energy level, they're driven, they're having a terrific time, they don't have the commitments on the family side that people in later stages of their life tend to have. There's a lot of "analysis paralysis" going on with a lot of these older guys because they didn't grow up that way. Only a couple of years ago we would only look at funding an entrepreneur who had done it before or had real operating experience.

Do you see your portfolio companies in a rush to develop internationally? How important is it for them to do this?

I was just at a board meeting with a relatively early-stage company in which we were discussing that. I think it's increasingly difficult to develop a presence in numerous countries until you have rounded out the management team and the business model. It's always been difficult, yet you have to look at it. Everyone knows they have to do something, but I think there's hesitancy on the part of most boards and most management teams when they look at it from afar to push too hard. I think generally the thought is that if you are going to do something on the international basis you have to find a well-funded partner who's local. I suspect that's why we're seeing some of the venture firms developing funds there such as CMGI and ICG. I think those firms are going to do great and they're in the right place to be.

Internet and technology companies obviously tend to grow very quickly in Internet time. As they grow extremely quickly how do you counsel your companies? What are the main things they need to remain focused on?

Not running out of cash. Most of these companies aren't making any money so they're not generating cash for the most part. So there's always going to be the issue of the next round of financing. The other thing they need to remain focused on is monitoring their business model. There has to be a real business there. There can't just be a great story or wonderful people. There has to be a real business that's going to make money.

Do you think we're at a point where we're poised for even greater growth due to new Internet and technology ventures?

I don't know where we are but we're not at the end. And we've only begun to see the tip of the iceberg with respect to some of the great value and leverage of the Internet and technologies that are available today

Tell me about some companies that you admire.

You can admire a company that has done a good job for five years but I think in order to really appreciate a company you have to look at it for a longer period of time. Microsoft, Cisco, Intel, and EMC are all companies I admire. Outside of the technology world I also admire companies like GE and Merck that have been around for a long time. All of those companies I think you have to admire because they survived and they've built value for their shareholders over a long period of time.

MARK LOTKE
Internet Capital Group

Mark Lotke brings over four years of experience as a private equity investor in Internet, software, and related information technology services companies and is the Managing Director in the Boston office of Internet Capital Group. Prior to joining ICG, Mark worked for General Atlantic Partners where he invested over $250 million in 10 companies, including E*Trade, Priceline.com, LHS Group, Envoy, NewSub Services, and Predictive Systems.

ICG partner companies include Animated Images, Arbinet, Autovia, BidCom, BuyMedia.com, Collabria, Commerx, ComputerJobs.com, CourtLink, CyberCrop.com, Deja.com, e-Chemicals, eMerge Interactive, Employeelife.com, Internet Commerce Systems, iParts, JusticeLink, Logistics.com, Metalsite.com, PaperExchange.com, PlanSponsor Exchange, RetailExchange.com, StarCite, Universal Access, USgift.com, assetTrade.com, eMarketWorld, ICG Commerce, NetVendor, Onvia.com, Residential Delivery Service, VerticalNet, Vivant!, Benchmarking Partners, Context Integration, US Interactive, Blackboard, ClearCommerce, Entegrity Solutions, ServiceSoft Technologies, Syncra Systems, Tradex Technologies, Breakaway Solutions, CommerceQuest, The LinkShare Corporation, PrivaSeek,

SageMaker, Sky Alland Marketing, Traffic.com, and United Messaging.

Take me through your background and how you ended up at Internet Capital Group.

I am a Wharton graduate and got into strategy consulting with a firm that spun out of Bain & Company back in 1983 called Corporate Decisions, Inc. (CDI). I then joined a private equity firm specializing in information technology called General Atlantic Partners where I focused on investing in vertical and horizontal client/server applications companies both domestically and in Europe. Next I went to Stanford Business school and returned to General Atlantic where I focused on IT services companies and business-to-consumer Internet companies such as E*Trade and Priceline. By late 1998, I realized that the next wave of new company formation would be in the business-to-business e-commerce space. Unfortunately, General Atlantic's investment philosophy was moving toward later staged companies and larger investments, which was not the sweet spot for business-to-business e-commerce action. At that time, and increasingly so today, it was clear that ICG was the best-positioned company to capitalize on the market opportunity. After meeting everybody in the ICG senior management team, I was sucked into the contagious enthusiasm and joined ICG to head up Acquisitions in their Boston office.

What do you find as the most exciting part about what you are doing now?

Working with our partner companies who are truly changing the face of business. We are running at laser speed and there is no time to sleep because it is a land grab like the Wild West. The business-to-business e-commerce book is being written real-time and I couldn't think of anything more exciting than being in the center of it.

Tell me about the investment philosophy of Internet Capital Group.

Our philosophy is incredibly focused, which is one of the keys to our success. We only invest in business-to-business e-commerce companies, which makes ICG an ideal partner because of our deep expertise. However, within business-to-business, we are stage agnostic, meaning we'll incubate companies, support companies in seed rounds, follow on rounds, pre-IPO, or where appropriate acquire a large stake in a public company. We proactively target the top 50 business-to-business markets and determine who is the best-positioned company to dominate the market. If no one exists we'll assembled the pieces of the pie to execute what we refer to internally as the "game over" strategy. We define business-to-business e-commerce rather broadly. A lot of our early investments were in infrastructure service providers, which might be software companies, IT services companies, or hosting companies, in essence the enablers or arms dealers for business-to-business e-commerce. Examples include Breakaway Solutions, TradeEx, and most recently Rightworks. Then we started acquiring interests in vertical market makers, which are exchanges and or marketplaces that bring together buyers and sellers in a certain vertical industry, such as MetalSite, PlasticsNet, and

PaperExchange We are also aggressively acquiring positions in horizontal market makers, which automate business processes that cut across the vertical markets, such as Logistics.com and E-Credit. We have also focused on customer aggregators such as VerticalNet for industrial communities and Onvia for the elusive small business sector.

What types of specific things do you like to see in the companies you invest in?

First, before we even delve into the company specific issues, we take a macro view on the market opportunity. Is this a large sector? Is this a sector that has a broken supply chain that could be improved with an e-commerce solution? We have a captive in house strategy group staffed by people from McKinsey, Bain, and Andersen who have identified the top 50 sectors of the economy that lend themselves to a business-to-business solution. Each quarter, we identify high priority sectors and assemble "hunting parties," drawing upon ICG resources from acquisitions, strategy, and operations to try and figure out what the winning models are for each of the sectors. Then we meet with numerous companies that are trying to solve that industry problem. In an ideal world, we find a leading company that is poised to dominate on a global basis. Frequently it's not that simple, such that it takes pulling together several companies with point solutions or approaching major incumbents and pulling them into the solution. So first we take a sector specific approach instead of a company specific approach, but for a particular company we look for a comprehensive solution, leadership position, and early traction, which may come in the form of inventory, actual transaction volume, or strategic partnerships.

What are some of the specifics you are looking for in a management team that you want to back?

First and foremost domain expertise is crucial. This is not business-to-consumer where Jeff Bezos of Amazon.com did not have to run a bookstore to take the industry by storm. If someone tried to pull off a vertical market maker in chemicals and did not come from the industry, the venture would be dead on arrival. Domain expertise is crucial, along with having a broad vision, the ability to execute, and a desire and passion to change the world. The management team however does not have to be complete. Ideally, you love it when the company has the long-term CEO and five or six direct reports, but that's not critical because we have 20+ full time executive recruiters who do nothing but searches on behalf of our partner companies.

How hard has it become for your partner companies to get the right people in a time when experienced human capital is so competitive to get?

It's crucial, but not difficult because of our unique operating model. Every company talks about it's limiting resource to growth is it's ability to find good people. This is often true, but if you peel back the onion, much of the time the real limiting resource is the company's ability to access strong search talent. Great employees are out there.

It's the search firms that have become the bottleneck. Not enough talented people have gone into IT search. By bringing the function in house, we have been able to cherry pick the best people in the recruiting business from Heidrick & Struggles, Korn Ferry, and Russell Reynolds and focus them as a captive search firm within ICG exclusively serving our partner companies. ICG is all about speed and providing every advantage possible to our partner companies to make sure they end up number one in their winner take most markets.

How important is it for companies you invest in to have some sort of proprietary technology?

Of course if you are an infrastructure service provider and you are offering a solution for a specific software space clearly you better be best-of-breed and have proprietary technology. However, most of our partner companies do not create technology. Instead, they use it. The key to business-to-business e-commerce is leveraging and integrating other provider's enabling technologies to solve an industry pain. I'd rather have a proprietary understanding of what is required for a world-class business-to-business solution, proprietary strategic partnerships, or proprietary access to leading buyers or sellers.

Why does ICG focus only on the business-to-business e-commerce space?

ICG was founded in 1996 with an exclusive focus on business-to-business e-commerce. From day one, Buck and Ken were convinced that business-to-business would dwarf the value creation we saw in business-to-consumer. The early days were lonely as much of the activity was in creating powerful business-to-consumer brands, but clearly our founders made a smart call. ICG believes that in order to be world class at something you need to focus exclusively on it. Because business-to-business is all we've done for the past four years, we've developed a deep understanding of the issues business-to-business companies face. Our partner companies value this expertise and we are able to leverage this knowledge across our network of partner companies. Many traditional venture firms that invest broadly in IT have made a handful of investments in business-to-business companies, but we have 60 business-to-business companies in our network. Business-to-business is all we do. We have 90 people that wake up every morning thinking about business-to-business.

How actively are you encouraging your partner companies to begin developing internationally?

Very, very active. We opened our London office five months ago and we opened up a Munich office this month. We have 15 people in Europe and will scale to 35 people in the next couple of months. ICG Europe will mirror the structure in the U.S. with employees focused on acquisitions, operations, strategy, recruiting, technology and finance so that we can support our partner companies. . Earlier this month we launched in Asia as well. We always knew that the business-to-business e-commerce opportunity is global by definition, but have been surprised how quickly the global phenomenon is developing.

Do you see any European dot coms as a threat to any business-to-business e-commerce niches where US based dot coms have already entered?

I think that the U.S. is more mature from a business-to-business e-commerce perspective because of the number of companies participating in the various verticals and the maturity of those business models. Because so many of the large and attractive sectors in the U.S. are very competitive, it is unlikely for a European company to threaten the U.S dot coms. More likely, we expect to see the U.S. companies entering the European markets, both organically and through M&A. However, just transplanting the U.S. models in Europe is not a recipe for success. Successful entrants will need to tweak their business models to adapt to the unique structure of many of the European markets. In addition, U.S. companies will need to build local management teams and partner with local incumbents in order to be successful. Increasingly as the U.S. business-to-business players go public and have access to a valuable paper currency, M&A activity with new European entrants will pick-up. Similarly, European dot coms that gain traction will pick-off smaller U.S. players to gain a foothold in the U.S. markets.

How has the business-to-business space matured to where it is today?

Although business-to-business is generating a tremendous amount of attention today, it has been quietly playing itself out over the last three years, moving from infrastructure service providers to vertical market makers to horizontal market makers and now industry specific e-procurement sites for Fortune 1000 companies. Over the past three to four years, the business-to-business pioneers have been marching their way through the largest sectors of the economy – steel, chemicals, plastics, pulp, and paper. All of the $200-$500 billion markets have been attacked, and in most of these sectors, the leaders are beginning to pull away from the pack. It sounds bizarre, but many of the new companies we see are targeting what people refer to as niche $10-$50 billion markets. Even though much of the U.S. land grab is over, we are only in the second inning in terms of value creation. The next business-to-business wave appears to be consolidation within specific vertical industries and then M&A across tangential industries.

What sort of business models in your space do you think will end up being the most profitable over time?

I like the vertically-oriented market makers. Specifically those business models that offer a holistic solution to an industry. Obviously this includes content, community, and commerce and much of the value creation will come from commerce. But it's also about collaboration, people coming together to do work, and the intersection between ASP software and exchanges. The best business models are not just about the buying and selling goods online and disintermediating wholesalers. Someone still must physically move the goods around the world. Therefore, integrated logistics solutions are critical. In addition, to complete a transaction online, sellers need credit verification services and buyers may want financing options. As a result, vertical market makers that integrate these additional services at the point of sale will increase online adoption and are well positioned to generate additional fees. The vertical market makers who provide industry leading solutions will create very large and profitable business with recurring revenue characteristics and desirable network economics.

Tell me about a company that you admire?

I strongly admire MetalSite. Besides being an early entrant in the online steel industry, MetalSite was visionary in it's understanding of the importance of bringing together large suppliers as equity participants. Some of their early competitors claimed to be more "neutral" but suffered from lack of supply, making their sites less compelling to buyers. Today, it has become more common for large industry buyers and sellers to launch exchanges such as the case with auto and retail, but MetalSite and particularly Weirton Steel were pioneers in this technique.

How much of a role in structuring the Internet economy have venture capitalists had?

At the end of the day, it really comes from the entrepreneurs. The VCs are enablers. Sure the VCs provide capital and the really good ones provide great strategic insight and a roll up their sleeves of attitude, but it's the entrepreneurs that make it happen day in and day out. At ICG, our operating model, scale, and focus allows us to offer resources and capabilities the VCs are not structured to provide, but it's our partner companies who are structuring and restructuring the Internet economy. ICG exists to serve our partner companies. They are our customers. We just help them run fast faster.

Tell me about the roll you play within your partner companies, or one in particular?

One example is a company we created called Logistics.com. It is a transportation exchange initially targeting the domestic trucking industry. Logistics.com is a company we created with Dr. Yossi Sheffi, the Director of the Transportation Center at MIT and an ICG Advisory Board Member. We developed the idea with Yossi and bought a business from Sabre Logistics to turbo charge the operations and gain access to some of the state-of-the-art carrier/shipper optimization and contracting tools. ICG was a founding shareholder in the company and over the past several months we have helped build out a world-class management team and are aggressively expanding the scope from trucking to multi-modal transportation through internal development and a series of partnerships.

How much interaction and partnering do you encourage between your partner companies?

This is the crux of the ICG model - the power of the network. Our partner companies interact significantly, both on their own and through organized events such as our market maker conferences, CFO conferences, sales and marketing conferences, and technology conferences to share best-demonstrated practices and avoid prior mistakes. Because our partner companies do not compete, they are very open to sharing ideas. For example, Emerge, a cattle and livestock market maker is never going to enter PlasticsNet's market, but much of the business models, partnership structures, and strategic issues they face are the similar. There is a lot of shared learning across our network. Partnerships between are companies are not mandated, but naturally develop with great frequency. In fact, it's an operating metric ICG tracks and measures ourselves. Many of our infrastructure services companies sell enabling technologies to our market makers and there are great synergies between our horizontal and vertical market makers. Interestingly, several recent partner companies encouraged ICG to acquire an interest in them despite the fact that they were adequately capitalized because these companies wanted access to our partner company network.

Do you think we are going to be in a land grab stage for many more years to come?

Not in the U.S. I think it is over in 12-18 months in terms of backing the best companies in the most attractive sectors of the economy. Fortunately, many of our market makers are leading their respective markets and value will accrue to the winners for well over a decade. However, outside the U.S., we see a completely different landscape where the land grab is just beginning. We are very optimistic about the opportunities in Europe and Asia.

What effect do you think a market crash would have on the wave of new ventures being started?

Not to dismiss the question, but I really don't think about the stock market. All I think about is what are the key sectors of the economy that lend themselves to a business-to-business solution? What are the components of an industry winning solution? Which company is best positioned to win? How can ICG work with that company to build a global dominator? Of course, the stock markets will have an effect on when a company is able to go public, but frankly this is irrelevant to ICG because we buy in the IPO and our exit strategy is not to have one. We are obsessed with building great long-term businesses that we want to own 15 to 20 years from now. Because ICG is an operating company and not a VC firm we do not have to return capital in order to raise the next fund. We have no fund. Our shareholders are IBM, GE, Compaq, Ford, and AT&T. So, a market correction is really a non-issue for us. However, a market crash would increase the cost of capital to new ventures by decreasing valuations, but I don't think it would slow up innovation or new company creation. Business-to-business e-commerce is a fundamental shift in the economy.

What advice would you give an entrepreneur starting a business-to-business e-commerce company?

First of all, make sure you or at least several members of your team come from the industry you are trying to serve. Secondly, pick an open market because first mover advantage is important, and lastly go for a comprehensive industry solution. If you don't, your competitor will beat you at the larger game.

ORDER THESE OTHER GREAT BOOKS TODAY!

Inside the Minds Series

Inside the Minds: Internet CFOs

Information Every Entrepreneur, Employee, Investor, and Services Professional Should Know About the Financial Side of Internet Companies – *Inside the Minds: Internet CFOs* includes interviews with leading CFOs from some of the top Internet companies in the world. Their research, advice, and experiences provide an unprecedented look at the financial side of Internet companies for entrepreneurs, employees, investors, and services professionals. Also examined are the way Internet companies are valued today and in the future, stock options, and financial trends affecting Internet companies at every level. *Inside the Minds: Internet CFOs* contains the most up to date information from leading industry professionals regarding the financial side of Internet companies available anywhere. (May 2000) $27.95

Inside the Minds: Internet Bigwigs

Industry Experts Forecast the Future of the Internet Economy - *Inside the Minds: Internet Bigwigs* includes interviews with a handful of the leading minds of the Internet and technology revolution. These individuals include Wall St. Analysts, Investment Bankers, Media Titans, CEOs and others. Their research, advice, and experiences provide an unprecedented look at the future of the Internet economy for executives, entrepreneurs, employees, and anyone worldwide who is interested in the Internet and technology revolution. Items discussed include killer-apps for the 21st century, stock market effects, emerging industries, key indicators to watch, international opportunities, and a plethora of other issues affecting anyone with a "vested interest" in the Internet and technology revolution. *Inside the Minds: Internet Bigwigs* contains the most up to date information from leading executives regarding the future of the Internet available anywhere (June 2000) $27.95

Inside the Minds: Internet Marketing

Industry Experts Reveal the Secrets to Marketing, Advertising, and Building a Successful Brand on the Internet - *Inside the Minds: Internet Marketing* includes interviews with leading marketing executives from some of the top Internet companies in the world. Their experiences, advice, and stories provide an unprecedented look at the various online and offline strategies involved with building a successful brand on the Internet for companies in every industry. Also examined is calculating return on investment, taking an offline brand online, taking an online brand offline, where the future of Internet marketing is heading, and numerous other issues. *Inside the Minds: Internet Marketing* contains the most up to date information available regarding online marketing and is a must have for anyone in the marketing, advertising, or public relations world. (May 2000) $27.95

Inside the Minds: Internet BizDev

Industry Experts Reveal the Secrets to Inking Deals in the Internet Industry - *Inside the Minds: Internet BizDev* includes interviews with leading business development executives from some of the top Internet companies in the world. Their experiences, advice, and stories provide an unprecedented look at the various strategies used to grow an Internet business, or Internet aspect of a business, for companies of every size and in every industry. Also examined are calculating potential return on investment, partnership strategies, joint ventures, and where the future of Internet business development is heading among numerous other issues. *Inside the Minds: Internet BizDev* contains the most up to date information available regarding business development and is a must have for every executive, entrepreneur, and anyone in the business development or marketing world. (May 2000) $27.95

Inside the Minds: Internet Lawyers
The Most Up to Date Handbook of Important Answers to Issues Facing Every Entrepreneur, Lawyer, and Anyone with a Web Site – *Inside the Minds: Internet Lawyers* includes interviews with leading lawyers from some of the top Internet and technology focused law firms in the world. Their research and advice provide the most up to date information available on legal issues reshaping the laws that govern the Internet and anyone who uses it. Also examined are topics such as structuring ownership, raising money, venture capital, patents, intellectual property, forming the board, product liability, human resources, going public, stock options, partnership contracts, privacy, and other issues that every business (and their lawyers) should be aware of. *Inside the Minds: Internet Lawyers* contains the most up to date legal information available anywhere and is a must have for every entrepreneur, lawyer, and anyone with a web site. (June 2000) $27.95

Inside the Minds: Chief Technology Officers
Industry Experts Reveal the Secrets to Developing, Implementing, and Capitalizing on the Best Technologies in the World - *Inside the Minds: Chief Technology Officers* includes interviews with leading technology executives from some of the top Internet and technology companies in the world. Their experiences, advice, and research provide an unprecedented look at the various strategies involved with developing, implementing, and capitalizing on the best technologies in the world for companies of every size and in every industry. These experts also provide insider knowledge on the future technologies that will once again reshape the "wired world." *Inside the Minds: Chief Technology Officers* contains the most up to date information available and is a must have for every techie, entrepreneur, executive, and any one with an interest in the technology fueling the Internet and technology revolution. (June 2000) $27.95

The Entire Inside the Minds Series
The Most Comprehensive Set of Industry Experts Ever Reveal the Secrets
Inside the Minds: Venture Capitalists
Inside the Minds: Internet CFOs
Inside the Minds: Internet Bigwigs
Inside the Minds: Internet Marketing
Inside the Minds: Internet Bizdev
Inside the Minds: Internet Lawyers
Inside the Minds: Chief Technology Officers
(May, June 2000) $195.65

ORDER THESE OTHER GREAT BOOKS TODAY!

Great for Yourself or Send as a Gift to Someone Else!

Tear Out This Page and Mail or Fax To:

eBrandedBooks.com, PO Box 883, Bedford, MA 01730
or
Fax to (617) 249-1970

Name:

Email:

Shipping Address:

City: State: Zip:

Billing Address:

City: State: Zip:

Phone:

Internet Marketing: Venture Capitalists: Internet Bigwigs:

Internet CFOs: Internet :Lawyers: Internet BizDev:

Chief Technology Officers: Entire Series:

Total Number of Books (an entire series is counted as one):

Credit Card Type (Visa & Mastercard ONLY):

Credit Card Number:

Expiration Date:

Signature:

*(Please note the billing address much match the address on file with your credit card company exactly)

Please make sure to provide your email address!

We shall send a confirmation receipt to your email address. Shipping and handling charges of $3.95 per book and appropriate state tax charges will be applied. All books are paperback and will be shipped as soon as they become available. Sorry, no returns or refunds. Books that are not already published will be shipped upon publication date. Publication dates are subject to delay.

Special Thanks

A special thanks to all the individuals that made this book possible:

Michael Moritz, Heidi Roizen, Jan Henric Buettner, Alex Wilmerding, Andrew Filipowski, Suzanne King, Jonathan Goldstein, Virginia Bonker, Guy Bradley, Stephen Andriole, Marc Benson, Roger Novak, Jack Biddle, Nuri Wissa, and Mark Lotke.

Thank you for sharing your knowledge and wisdom with the rest of the world.

Special thanks also to:

Melissa Conradi, L. Adrienne Wichard, and Jack at Sowa & Nichols Printing

Venture Capital Access Online (www.vcaonline.com)
VCAOnline.com is a venture capital and private equity marketplace on the Internet where entrepreneurs can raise capital for their businesses, investors can find new deals, and advisors can contact potential clients. VCAOnline.com also publishes an electronic venture capital directory, VCPro Database, which includes 3,000 venture-financing sources worldwide.

VentureDirectory.com (www.venturedirectory.com)
VentureDirectory.com is a leading financial site on the Internet that lists deals and invites selected pre-qualified capital sources to visit. VentureDirectory.com also lists companies for sale and acquisition interests in addition to having a special business opportunities section for smaller businesses. VentureDirectory.com also has a special area for those having substantial experience in investment banking, corporate finance, commercial banking, major business brokerage, and business plan writing where they can interact with other individuals, receive information on new financial sources, and be the first to see new deals.

eBrandedBooks.com

Presents the

INSIDE THE MINDS SERIES

Inside the Minds: Venture Capitalists is the first book in the Inside the Minds Series. Other books currently include *Internet CFOs, Internet Marketing, Internet BizDev, Internet Bigwigs, Chief Technology Officers,* and *Internet Lawyers.* The series was conceived in order to give individuals worldwide actual insights into the leading minds of the Internet and technology revolution. Because individuals in this industry especially are so busy and the nature of their business is changing so quickly, there exist very few books that are published in a timely enough manner and written by individuals actually in industry. eBrandedBooks.com is now expanding the series to share the wealth of knowledge locked inside the minds of leading executives in every industry worldwide.

To nominate yourself or an executive level individual for an upcoming book in the Inside the Minds Series please email jennifer@ebrandedbooks.com. We are currently accepting nominations for executives worldwide in every major industry.

About eBrandedBooks.com

eBrandedBooks.com is the first ever print and electronic publisher to offer a free publishing solution for individuals and businesses worldwide. Individuals can publish a book, newsletter, article, group story, diary, research report, short story, play, and notes on any topic via the eBrandedBooks.com web site. eBrandedBooks.com acts as their personal agent and publisher: publishing their work electronically on eBrandedBooks.com, getting their work listed in other electronic marketplaces, promoting it with extensive advertising and affiliate programs, and simplifying the entire process for them. And if their work is purchased on eBrandedBooks.com 100 times, eBrandedBooks.com will edit, print publish, and help get it into bookstores and other retail outlets nationwide either as its own book or combined with other shorter works. eBrandedBooks.com also works with companies to help them write books, establish their own private label book publishing arms, and harness the written works of their community members. eBrandedBooks.com also publishes the highly acclaimed Inside the Minds series, Gold Digger series, and CEO series. For more information on becoming an eBrandedBooks.com business partner please email jonp@ebrandedbooks.com. For more information on becoming a published author please register at www.ebrandedbooks.com.

9 781587 620010